REVISE AQA GCSE
Spanish

REVISION WORKBOOK

Series Consultant: Harry Smith

Authors: Leanda Reeves and Tracy Traynor

Also available to support your revision:

Revise GCSE Study Skills Guide   9781447967071

The **Revise GCSE Study Skills Guide** is full of tried-and-trusted hints and tips for how to learn more effectively. It gives you techniques to help you achieve your best – throughout your GCSE studies and beyond!

Revise GCSE Revision Planner   9781447967828

The **Revise GCSE Revision Planner** helps you to plan and organise your time, step-by-step, throughout your GCSE revision. Use this book and wall chart to mastermind your revision.

For the full range of Pearson revision titles across GCSE, BTEC and AS Level visit:
www.pearsonschools.co.uk/revise

PEARSON

Contents

LIFESTYLE
1   Birthdays
2   Pets
3   Physical description
4   Character description
5   Brothers and sisters
6   Extended family
7   Friends
8   Daily routine
9   Breakfast
10 Eating at home
11 Eating in a café
12 Eating in a restaurant
13 Healthy eating
14 Keeping fit and healthy
15 Health problems
16 Future relationships
17 Social issues
18 Social problems

LEISURE
19 Hobbies
20 Sport
21 Arranging to go out
22 Last weekend
23 TV programmes
24 Cinema
25 Music
26 New technology
27 Internet language
28 Internet pros and cons
29 Shops
30 Shopping for food
31 At the market
32 Clothes and colours
33 Shopping for clothes
34 Returning items
35 Shopping opinions
36 Pocket money
37 Holiday destinations
38 Holiday accommodation
39 Booking accommodation
40 Staying in a hotel
41 Staying on a campsite
42 Holiday activities
43 Holiday preferences
44 Future holiday plans
45 Holiday experiences

HOME AND ENVIRONMENT
46 Countries and nationalities
47 My house
48 My room
49 Helping at home
50 My neighbourhood
51 Places in town
52 At the tourist office
53 Things to do in town
54 Signs around town
55 Where I live
56 Town description
57 Weather
58 Celebrations at home
59 Directions
60 Transport
61 At the train station
62 News headlines
63 The environment
64 Environmental issues
65 What I do to be 'green'

WORK AND EDUCATION
66 School subjects
67 School description
68 School routine
69 Comparing schools
70 At primary school
71 Rules at school
72 Problems at school
73 Future education plans
74 Future plans
75 Jobs
76 Job adverts
77 CV
78 Job application
79 Job interview
80 Opinions about jobs
81 Part-time jobs
82 My work experience
83 Work experience
84 Dialogues and messages

GRAMMAR
85   Nouns and articles
86   Adjectives
87   Possessives and pronouns
88   Comparisons
89   Other adjectives
90   Pronouns
91   The present tense
92   Reflexives and irregulars
93   *Ser* and *estar*
94   The gerund
95   The preterite tense
96   The imperfect tense
97   The future tense
98   The conditional
99   Perfect and pluperfect
100 Giving instructions
101 The present subjunctive
102 Negatives
103 Special verbs
104 *Por* and *para*
105 Questions and exclamations
106 Connectives and adverbs
107 Numbers
108 **Practice Exam Paper: Reading**
115 **Practice Exam Paper: Listening**
119 **Answers**

Audio files

Audio files and transcripts for the listening exercises in this book can be found at: www.pearsonschools.co.uk/mflrevisionaudio

---

A small bit of small print

AQA publishes Sample Assessment Material and the Specification on its website. This is the official content and this book should be used in conjunction with it. The questions in this book have been written to help you practise what you have learned in your revision. Remember: the real exam questions may not look like this.

Target grades

Target grades are quoted in this book for some of the questions. Students targeting this grade should be aiming to get some of the marks available. Students targeting a higher grade should be aiming to get all of the marks available.

Birthdays

1 When were they born?

When were these people born? Write the correct letter in each box.

A Alejandro

> Yo nací el catorce de enero.

B Víctor

> Celebro mi cumple el once de diciembre. Este año voy a cumplir quince años.

C María

> Mi cumpleaños es el quince de julio. Siempre lo celebro con mi familia.

D Gloria

> Mi cumpleaños es el siete de junio, el día después del cumpleaños de mi hermano.

E Fran

> Mi fecha de nacimiento es el ocho de marzo de mil novecientos noventa y siete.

F Juan

> Nací el doce de octubre.

Example: January ┌─────┐ A ┌─────┐

(a) March   ┌ E ┐   *(1 mark)*

(b) June   ┌ D ┐   *(1 mark)*

(c) July   ┌ C ┐   *(1 mark)*

(d) December ┌ B ┐   *(1 mark)*

(e) October   ┌ F ┐   *(1 mark)*

2 My birthday

> **Audio files**
> Audio files can be found at:
> www.pearsonschools.co.uk/mflrevisionaudio

Listen to these people talking about their birthdays.

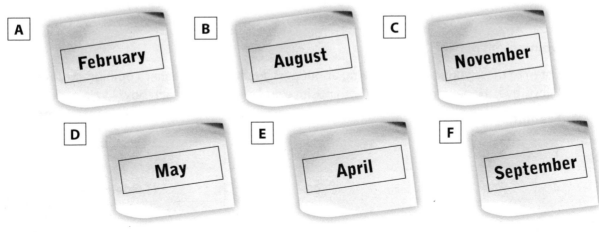

Write the correct letter in each box.

1 ☐ *(1 mark)*   **2** ☐ *(1 mark)*   **3** ☐ *(1 mark)*   **4** ☐ *(1 mark)*

Pets

3 Talking about pets

Look at the pictures of pets.

| A | B | C | D |

| E | F | G | H |

> Where there are pictures, think about the vocabulary you know which could match with them.

Which pet is each person talking about? Write the correct letter in the box.

(a) Quiero un caballo negro.	
(b) Tengo un pequeño perro blanco muy bonito.	
(c) Tengo un conejo gris que se llama Fifi.	
(d) No me gusta el ratón gris de mi hermano.	

(1 mark)

(1 mark)

(1 mark)

(1 mark)

> Make sure you look for the **key** vocabulary in the sentences.

4 Opinions on pets

Listen to these young people talking about pets. Identify the speaker's opinion, writing **P** (positive), **N** (negative) or **P/N** (both positive and negative) in each box.

Example: P

1 ☐ *(1 mark)*   3 ☐ *(1 mark)*

2 ☐ *(1 mark)*   4 ☐ *(1 mark)*

Physical description

5 My brother

Read Jorge's letter about his brother.

> ¡Hola, Roberto!
>
> ¿Quieres saber algo sobre mi hermano Raúl?
>
> Es mi único hermano. Es menor que yo, pero parece mayor. Es un chico simpático. Dicen que se parece a mí, pero yo no lo creo. Raúl es muy alto. No es ni gordo ni delgado, pero está bastante fuerte y le gusta ir al gimnasio. Lleva gafas y dicen que es guapo. Es verdad que tenemos el mismo pelo rizado, largo y castaño, pero él lleva coleta y yo no. Yo suelo llevar el pelo suelto. Se parece más a mi madre que a mi padre.
>
> En tu próxima carta dime cómo es tu hermana mayor. ¿Te llevas bien con ella?
>
> ¡Hasta luego!
>
> Jorge

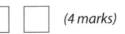

Remember to skim and scan for key words you recognise, which might help you.

Which **four** sentences are correct? Write the correct letter in each box.

A	Jorge's brother is called Raúl.
B	He is older than Jorge.
C	He doesn't have a good opinion of him.
D	He is good-looking.
E	He looks strong.
F	He is younger than he looks.

G	He has Jorge's eyes.
H	He has Jorge's hair.
I	He has the same hairstyle.

Example: ☐ A

☐ ☐ ☐ ☐   *(4 marks)*

6 What do they do look like?

Listen to these young people describing others. Choose the best description for each person.

A	thin and ugly	F	tall and fat
B	fat and good looking	G	long hair and blue eyes
C	tall and wears glasses	H	short hair and blue eyes
D	tall and has an earring	I	red hair and green eyes
E	tall and thin	J	red hair and wears glasses

Write the correct letter in each box.

Example: Felicia ☐ G

1   Miguel   ☐   *(1 mark)*   3   Gloria   ☐   *(1 mark)*

2   Félix   ☐   *(1 mark)*   4   Borjita ☐   *(1 mark)*

3

Character description

7 Teo's autobiography homework

Part A

Read what Teo has written.

> Me llamo Teo Mateus Sidrón. Soy muy estudioso en el cole y saco buenas notas. Antes era un poco maleducado, pero ahora siempre me porto muy bien. Me encantan los deportes. Paso mucho tiempo jugando al baloncesto y soy miembro del equipo de vela. Es muy importante estar en forma. En el futuro, tengo la intención de ir a la universidad para estudiar Empresariales. Mi mejor amigo, Pablo, es más atrevido que yo – a veces, soy un poco tímido – pero estoy seguro de que ganaré mucho dinero. Creo que todo es posible si trabajas mucho.

According to Teo, which **four** of the following words describe his character? Write the correct letter in each box.

A	hardworking
B	rude
C	honest
D	intelligent
E	lazy

F	fit
G	daring
H	shy
I	ambitious

Example: A

☐ ☐ ☐ ☐   *(4 marks)*

Part B

Teo goes on to talk about people. Read what he says.

> Con respecto a los amigos, soy muy particular y espero mucho de ellos. No hay nada más importante que llevarnos bien. Creo que hay que tratar a los demás con respeto. No aguanto a la gente antipática o maleducada. La verdad es que me gustan las personas divertidas porque para mí, es muy importante que alguien me haga reír. También me gusta la gente que es habladora. Sin embargo, no tengo tiempo para los mentirosos o los que sólo piensan en sí mismos.

What **four** types of people does he talk about? Write the correct letter in each box.

A	respectful
B	extroverts
C	selfish
D	funny
E	serious

F	talkative
G	naughty
H	unkind
I	rude

Example: A

☐ ☐ ☐ ☐   *(4 marks)*

> Underline key words in the text to help you. Thinking of synonyms (words that mean the same thing) can help you work out tricky language.

Brothers and sisters

8 Julián's e-mail

Read this e-mail from a possible penfriend.

> ¡Hola!
>
> Me llamo Julián. Tengo catorce años y tengo una hermana menor. Nos parecemos mucho, pero no me llevo bien con ella – ¡es tonta! Discutimos mucho.
>
> ¿Tienes hermanos?
>
> Saludos,
>
> Julián

What details are mentioned? Write the correct letter in each box.

Example: The boy is called …

A	Javi.
B	Raúl.
C	Julián.

C

(a) He is …

A	13 years old.
B	14 years old.
C	15 years old.

☐ *(1 mark)*

(b) His sister is …

A	the same age.
B	older.
C	younger.

☐ *(1 mark)*

(c) They look …

A	identical.
B	different.
C	alike.

☐ *(1 mark)*

(d) They get on …

A	badly.
B	well.
C	sometimes.

☐ *(1 mark)*

9 My roots

Listen to Juan talking about his family. What does he say about how he gets on with them?

A	his stepbrother

B	his father

C	his stepmother

D	his brothers

E	the whole family

F	his aunt

Write the correct letter in each box.

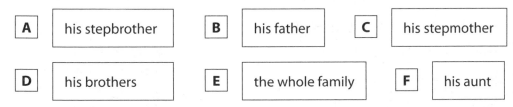

1	He gets on well with		*(1 mark)*
2	He shares the same interests with		*(1 mark)*

3	He argues with		*(1 mark)*
4	He used to get on badly with		*(1 mark)*

Extended family

10 Ana's family

Read what Ana says about her family. Identify the opinions expressed.

Write **P** (positive), **N** (negative) or **P + N** (both positive and negative) in each box.

Example: Mi tía es guapa.   P

A	Mi primo Paco es tonto.	☐ (1 mark)
B	Mi madrastra me hace reír, es divertida.	☐ (1 mark)
C	Me encanta mi hermano pequeño, Carlos, aunque puede ser muy desagradable.	☐ (1 mark)
D	¿Salir con mi hermana Susi? ¡No, gracias!	☐ (1 mark)
E	A mi tío le encanta el fútbol. ¡Qué aburrido!	☐ (1 mark)
F	Mi hermana mayor es simpática.	☐ (1 mark)
G	Mi padre es ruidoso.	☐ (1 mark)
H	Loli me ayuda con mis deberes. ¡Es guay!	☐ (1 mark)

11 My sister

Listen to Úrsula talking about her cousin, Marisol.

What **four** things does she say? Write the correct letters in the boxes.

A	Marisol is funny.
B	Sharing a room with Marisol is annoying.
C	Marisol doesn't live with her parents.
D	Marisol argues with her dad all the time.
E	Marisol uses Úrsula's things.
F	Marisol helps Úrsula with her homework.
G	Marisol gets on well with her stepmother.
H	Marisol likes the same kind of music as Úrsula.

- Take care to listen and make notes which will give you a little more time to find the answers.
- Listen for cognates and don't be afraid to make an intelligent guess – you might just get it right!

☐ ☐ ☐ ☐

(4 marks)

Friends

12 Marta's friends

Read what Marta has to say about her friends.

> Me llamo Marta y para mí la amistad es muy importante. Tengo tres amigos muy simpáticos. Antonio va al mismo colegio que yo y es como un hermano. A menudo jugamos con el ordenador. Isabel es muy tranquila. Cuando tengo un problema, me ayuda. Por ejemplo, cuando rompí con mi novio estaba allí para ayudarme. Hugo es muy gracioso. Me hace reír. Me acepta como soy y siempre está a mi lado.

According to Marta, which **three** of the following statements are true? Write the correct letters in the boxes.

A	She goes to school with Antonio.
B	Isabel has many problems.
C	Marta and Antonio are neighbours.
D	Hugo is funny.
E	Isabel is naughty.
F	Antonio is like a member of her family.

☐ ☐ ☐

(3 marks)

13 My best friend

Listen to Loli describing her friend Javier. Answer the questions **in English.**

(a) What examples does Loli give of Javier's generosity? Give **two** reasons.

  (i) .... *(1 mark)*

  (ii) .... *(1 mark)*

(b) In Loli's opinion, what characterises a good friend? Give **two** answers.

  (i) .... *(1 mark)*

  (ii) .... *(1 mark)*

(c) Why is it surprising that Javier does so well at school?

.... *(1 mark)*

(d) What did Javier achieve last season?

.... *(1 mark)*

(e) What is Loli going to do next week?

.... *(1 mark)*

Daily routine

14 Óscar's routine

Read this e-mail from Óscar and answer the questions **in English**.

○ ○ ○   ▭

🚫   ↩   ↩↩   →   🖨
Borrar   Responder   Responder   Adelante   Imprimir
                       a todas

¡Hola!

Hoy es lunes y como siempre, me desperté temprano, a las seis y cuarto, para ir al cole. Primero me lavé los dientes y después me puse unos vaqueros. Como hacía buen tiempo, decidí ir al cole a pie. Esta tarde intentaré relajarme porque, por una vez, no tengo deberes.

Óscar

Example: What day does Óscar refer to?

.... Monday ....

(a) What time did he get up? .... 6.15 ....   *(1 mark)*

(b) What did he wear to school? .. Jeans ....   *(1 mark)*

(c) How did he get to school? ... walking ....   *(1 mark)*

(d) What will he do this evening? . relax ....   *(1 mark)*

(e) Why will he do this? ... He has no homework .. *(1 mark)*

> Read **all** the questions before you start so you don't give too much information in an earlier answer.

15 A typical morning

Listen to Roque talk about a typical day. Answer the questions **in English.**

Example: What part of the day does Roque refer to?

.... Mornings ....

(a) What's his opinion of school?

.... *(1 mark)*

(b) Why does he have to get up early?

.... *(1 mark)*

(c) What other activities form part of his daily routine? Give **two** details.

.... and .... *(2 marks)*

(d) Where does Roque have breakfast?

.... *(1 mark)*

Breakfast

16 What's for breakfast?

What can you buy for breakfast? Write the correct **four** letters in the boxes.

A   **B**

Cafetería Sol

Desayuno **3€**
fruta
cereales
zumo de naranja
té
tostadas
huevos
salchichas

C   **D**

E   **F**   **G**   **H**

E D A B

(4 marks)

17 Healthy eating

Alba is talking about a healthy living article she is reading. Note the **four** correct sentences.

A	The article says breakfast is quite important.
B	The article says breakfast does not have a big effect on health.
C	Alba is not surprised by the article.
D	Breakfast prepares you for anything.
E	The article lists academic success as a positive result of having breakfast.

F	The article describes the effects of not having breakfast.
G	The article tells you what to eat.
H	Alba is not convinced.
I	Alba is going to change her ways.

Write the **four** correct letters in the boxes.

☐ ☐ ☐ ☐

(4 marks)

Eating at home

18 Food preferences

Some young people are discussing food. Read and note their opinions. Write **P** (positive), **N** (negative) or **P + N** (both positive and negative) in each box.

> ¡Me <u>encanta</u> merendar!

Ana

> Yo prefiero el pollo con patatas fritas que hace mi padre. Prepara platos sabrosos ^{tasty} con especias e ingredientes exóticos. ¡En mi casa nos gusta el picante!

Gustavo

> Para mí, la comida más rica es la del domingo. Siempre tomamos chuletas o un buen pescado, y para mí, tienen que estar bien hechos. ¡Después de hacer deporte el domingo, siempre tenemos hambre! La comida que <u>menos</u> me gusta son los espaguetis.

Isabel

> ¡Lo que más me gusta son los postres! Me encantan los helados, las tartas y todo tipo de pastelería, ¡aunque sé que no son <u>nada</u> buenos para la salud! <u>Odio</u> la fruta.

Sofía

> Cocinar me lleva <u>demasiado</u> tiempo – para mí la comida es una necesidad – <u>no</u> algo que me guste.

Pablo

Example: Ana | P |

| 1 | Gustavo | P | *(1 mark)* |

| 2 | Isabel | P+N | *(1 mark)* |

| 3 | Sofía | P+N | *(1 mark)* |

| 4 | Pablo | N | *(1 mark)* |

19 Favourite food

Listen to these people talk about their favourite food. What do they like to eat?

| A | salad | C | fish | E | chicken |
| B | pasta | D | meat | F | chips |

Write the correct letter in each box.

Example: Artur | B |

| 1 | Dolores | | *(1 mark)* | 3 | Loli | | *(1 mark)* |
| 2 | Paco | | *(1 mark)* | 4 | Jorge | | *(1 mark)* |

Eating in a café

20 At the café

What do these people order? Write the correct food or drink **in English**.

> Quiero una limonada.

Chus

> Me apetece un zumo de naranja.

Elvira

> Para mí, agua sin gas.

Juan

> Yo quiero un bocadillo de jamón.

Fátima

> Voy a tomar un helado de vainilla.

Nando

Example: Chus .....lemonade.........................

1	Elvira	orange juice	(1 mark)
2	Juan	still water	(1 mark)
3	Fátima	ham sandwich	(1 mark)
4	Nando	vanilla ice cream	(1 mark)

21 Ordering drinks

Listen to these young people. What do they order?

A	tea
B	hamburger
C	apple juice
D	black coffee
E	glass of milk
F	piece of cake
H	Coca-Cola

Write the correct letter in each box.

Example: H

1 ☐ *(1 mark)*   2 ☐ *(1 mark)*   3 ☐ *(1 mark)*   4 ☐ *(1 mark)*

Eating in a restaurant

22 Eating out

Read what these people say about eating out.

Comer fuera – lo que me gusta y lo que no me gusta …

Marga: Me gusta experimentar y probar sabores diferentes.

Alejandro: No me gusta nada estar esperando mucho tiempo en los bares.

Juan: De vez en cuando la comida está demasiado salada.

Carmen: En los restaurantes de mi barrio los camareros son todos simpáticos.

Ricardo: ¡Anoche pedí un gazpacho de primer plato y no estaba frío!

What does each person refer to? Write the correct letter in each box.

A	new things
B	choice of food
C	being kept waiting
D	temperature of the food
E	cost

F	taste of the food
G	drinks
H	value for money
I	service

> Be careful – there are always some 'red herrings' and you can be easily misled by distractors.

Example: Marga   A

1   Alejandro   C   *(1 mark)*

2   Juan   F   *(1 mark)*

3   Carmen   I   *(1 mark)*

4   Ricardo   D   *(1 mark)*

23 At the restaurant

Listen to the dialogue at a restaurant. Write the correct letter in the box.

Example: He wants the …

A	bill.
B	menu.
C	wine list.

A

(a) They want to …

A	complain.
B	have dessert.
C	order.

(1 mark)

(c) They want …

A	to leave.
B	a discount.
C	to forget it.

(1 mark)

(b) They do this because …

A	the food was late.
B	the food was hot.
C	the food was cold.

(1 mark)

(d) The meal cost them …

A	30 euros.
B	25 euros.
C	40 euros.

(1 mark)

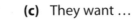

Healthy eating

24 Healthy diet

Look at these pictures of food.

| A | B | C | D | E | F |

Write the letter of the matching picture in each box.

Example: manzanas   A

(a) pasteles ☐ *(1 mark)*   **(c)** galletas ☐ *(1 mark)*

(b) nueces ☐ *(1 mark)*   **(d)** plátanos ☐ *(1 mark)*

25 Keeping healthy

What diet plans do the friends have? Why? Listen and complete the table **in English**.

Example:

Name	Plan	Reason
Ines	eat more fruit	because it is healthy

1

Name	Plan	Reason
Avelina		

(2 marks)

2

Name	Plan	Reason
Alfonso		

(2 marks)

3

Name	Plan	Reason
Carolina		

(2 marks)

4

Name	Plan	Reason
Juan		

(2 marks)

Had a go ☐ Nearly there ☐ Nailed it! ☐

Keeping fit and healthy

26 Staying healthy

Read this article about healthy lifestyles.

> Es un hecho bien conocido que para llevar una vida sana, es imprescindible mantenerse en forma haciendo ejercicio a diario. Hoy en día mucha gente tiene un entrenador personal para ayudarles con su régimen y con los ejercicios, pero la verdad es que no es necesario tener un entrenador y además, puede resultar bastante caro. Hacer un análisis simple de tu rutina diaria te puede ofrecer soluciones que no cuestan ni dinero ni tiempo. Por ejemplo, acostarte más temprano cada noche para leer un rato y relajarte puede traer un beneficio considerable. Al levantarte, deja tiempo para dar un paseo corto por el jardín.
>
> A pesar de lo que dicen muchos, un poco de estrés no es algo totalmente negativo – lo que sí es importante, es mantener una actitud positiva. Sugiero que hables con tu familia y amigos sobre lo que te preocupa, antes de que se convierta en un problema.
>
> Comer bien también es otro factor importante. No pasa nada por tomar comida basura, mientras no lo hagas todos los días y sigas una dieta equilibrada. Se supone que una bebida alcohólica de vez en cuando no te puede hacer daño, pero debes evitar fumar a toda costa.
>
> Es muy importante beber, por lo menos, dos vasos grandes de agua al día y tomar suficientes frutas y verduras.

What recommendations are made for maintaining a healthy lifestyle? Write notes under the following headings **in English**.

Example:

Diet
eat a balanced diet; can eat fast foot but not everyday

(a)

Exercise

(2 marks)

(b)

Changes to daily routine

(2 marks)

(c)

Stress

(2 marks)

(d)

Alcohol and smoking

(2 marks)

Health problems

27 Alcohol problems

Read this newspaper article.

> Apesar de que el alcoholismo afecta sobre todo a los adultos, el consumo de alcohol entre los adolescentes es cada vez más preocupante. Los últimos estudios científicos han identificado a los jóvenes en peligro de convertirse en alcohólicos, que se caracterizan por las siguientes tendencias:
> - Beben demasiado y con rapidez en las reuniones.
> - Aumenta su tolerancia al alcohol y la frecuencia con que beben.
> - Sufren dolores de cabeza y tienen la memoria dañada.
> - Empiezan a beber en secreto.
>
> Si tú o algún amigo tuyo hacéis algo semejante, puede significar que tenéis un problema. Buscad la ayuda y el consejo de vuestros padres, profesores o médicos.
> También se ha comprobado que el abuso del alcohol entre los jóvenes trae muchas consecuencias negativas como:
> - problemas con la familia y con los amigos
> - paranoia
> - agresividad y conducta antisocial
> - pérdida del trabajo y de las amistades
> - inseguridad.
>
> Y todo ello sin hablar de los efectos perjudiciales para los órganos principales del cuerpo.

Answer the following questions **in English**.

> Look for familiar words and use the context to try and work out what information the answer requires.

(a) What problem does the article describe?

.... *(1 mark)*

(b) Name **two** warning signs shown by young people who may be affected by the problem.

  (i) .... *(1 mark)*

  (ii) .... *(1 mark)*

(c) What advice is given to these young people?

.... *(1 mark)*

(d) Which **two** symptoms affecting young people's mental state are mentioned?

  (i) .... *(1 mark)*

  (ii) .... *(1 mark)*

(e) What other problems can be caused by the addiction? Name **two** of them.

  (i) .... *(1 mark)*

  (ii) .... *(1 mark)*

Future relationships

28 Future plans

Read the views of these three young people on marriage.

> **Natalia:** Me gustaría casarme algún día. Tengo novio desde hace tres años y estoy muy contenta. No sé si seguiremos juntos en el futuro, pero sé que quiero tener dos hijos. Creo que sería muy buena madre. La verdad es que no hablamos de eso.

> **Arturo:** No quiero casarme. Tengo miedo. Mis padres están divorciados y creo que me han dado muy mal ejemplo. Cuando era pequeño discutían todo el rato, lo que me ponía muy triste. Para mí, será mejor simplemente tener una pareja.

> **Lola:** Estoy enamorada de un chico a quien conocí hace tres meses en la boda de mi hermana mayor. Es superguapo, simpático y compartimos los mismos gustos. Ya estamos planeando unas vacaciones juntos. Algún día me gustaría casarme, pero no quiero tener hijos porque no tengo suficiente paciencia.

Who does each statement refer to? Write **N** (Natalia), **A** (Arturo) or **L** (Lola) in each box.

Example: Who does not want to marry?   ☐ A

(a) Who has been in a long-term relationship? ☐   *(1 mark)*

(b) Who is scared of marriage? ☐   *(1 mark)*

(c) Who does not want to have children? ☐   *(1 mark)*

(d) Who was sad when they were younger? ☐   *(1 mark)*

(e) Who has recently fallen in love? ☐   *(1 mark)*

(f) Who discusses the future with their partner? ☐   *(1 mark)*

(g) Who thinks they would be a good parent? ☐   *(1 mark)*

29 Future relationships

Listen to these three young people talking about future relationships. Complete the sentences below **in English**.

Example: Alicia thinks that .....personality.......................... is very important.

1. Leonardo would like to meet someone who is ....and thinks

   that...is unimportant.   *(2 marks)*

2. Mario would like to meet someone who is ....and thinks

   ....is unimportant.   *(2 marks)*

Social issues

30 Young people in Mexico

Read this extract from an article about young people in Mexico.

Siendo ya consciente de una pobreza general e inquietante entre la juventud de México, causada principalmente por el paro, la mayoría de las organizaciones internacionales están de momento más preocupadas por la actual cantidad de jóvenes traumatizados. Resulta que muchos chicos de edades entre 14 y 18 años viven aterrorizados por la violencia y el maltrato. Además, parece ser que la falta de empleo está forzando a muchos jóvenes a emigrar. Eso quiere decir que son más vulnerables todavía y que sufren por estar separados de sus familias, si es que la tienen. La desesperación que sienten les lleva al alcoholismo y a tomar drogas. El talento se está desperdiciando totalmente y se buscan soluciones con urgencia.

Answer these questions **in English.**

(a) What does the article say is a problem for young Mexicans?

.... *(1 mark)*

(b) What has made teenagers afraid?

.... *(1 mark)*

(c) What are many young people forced to do?

.... *(1 mark)*

(d) What effect does this have on them? Mention **two** things.

.... *(2 marks)*

(e) What are international organizations doing?

.... *(1 mark)*

31 Helping young people

Listen to Iker talking about his job. Answer the following questions **in English.**

(a) Why does Iker work with young people?

.... *(1 mark)*

(b) What has he found to be the most common problem?

.... *(1 mark)*

(c) What does he say about conflict between generations?

.... *(1 mark)*

(d) Name **two** consequences of a breakdown in communication.

(i) .... *(1 mark)*

(ii) .... *(1 mark)*

(e) Name **two** things the authorities might do if the situation gets really bad.

(i) .... **(ii)**.. *(2 marks)*

(f) Name **one** of the positive things Iker mentions often happens.

.... *(1 mark)*

17

Social problems

32 Guillermo's article

Read this article in which Guillermo shares his thoughts about the youth of today.

Me llamo Guillermo y me encanta mi vida siendo un joven del siglo XXI.

Creo que la mayoría de los jóvenes son buenas personas. Mi padre, sin embargo, no está de acuerdo. Siempre se enfada porque lee en los periódicos noticias en las que se habla de jóvenes drogadictos o gamberros. ¡Pero la prensa pinta una imagen negativa y estoy cansado de oír siempre lo mismo! Yo soy más optimista y sé que muchas personas jóvenes hacen una gran labor social. Mi madre dice que todos somos egoístas, pero yo no estoy de acuerdo. Pienso que sí nos preocupamos por los demás.

Además, tengo un amigo de dieciséis años que estudia, trabaja y también cuida de su abuelo de noventa años – y todo con una sonrisa. ¡Eso es maravilloso!

> Take care – the options are often similar and some will be misleading. This is why it is essential to read carefully. If you don't recognise all the vocabulary try using a process of elimination!

Answer the following questions, by writing the correct letter in each box.

Example: Guillermo thinks young people are …

A	frustrated
B	great.
C	wasting their time.

B

(a) His dad thinks young people are …

A	hooligans.
B	negative.
C	angry.

☐ *(1 mark)*

(b) Guillermo thinks the press is …

A	biased
B	optimistic.
C	wrong.

☐ *(1 mark)*

(c) His mum says young people are …

A	selfish.
B	charitable.
C	worried.

☐ *(1 mark)*

(d) Guillermo's friend looks after his grandfather …

A	grudgingly.
B	willingly.
C	occasionally.

☐ *(1 mark)*

33 What worries you?

Listen to these young people. What worries them?

A	bullying	C	terrorism	E	the economy	G	human rights
B	the homeless	D	social media	F	hooligans	H	the press

Write the correct letter in each box.

1   Alicia   ☐   *(1 mark)*   3   Trini   ☐   *(1 mark)*

2   Rodrigo   ☐   *(1 mark)*   4   Sandro   ☐   *(1 mark)*

Hobbies

1 My favourite hobby

Read the information on the blog.

A	B	C	D
Voy de pesca.	Voy al cine.	Juego al tenis los sábados.	Toco la guitarra.

E	F
Juego a los videojuegos con mis amigos.	Juego al ajedrez cada martes.

> In reading texts, look for words which are cognates (similar to English words).

Which blog has each person written? Write the correct letter in each box.

(a) Carlos likes racket sports. ☐ *(1 mark)*

(b) María prefers playing an instrument. ☐ *(1 mark)*

(c) Pablo loves board games. ☐ *(1 mark)*

(d) Esther likes computers. ☐ *(1 mark)*

2 An ideal weekend

Listen to these people talking about what they want to do.

A   B   C

> Study the rubric and pictures carefully and try to predict what you might hear.

D   E   F

Write the correct letter in each box.

1 Marta ☐ *(1 mark)*   **3** Pablo ☐ *(1 mark)*

2 Luis ☐ *(1 mark)*   **4** Cristina ☐ *(1 mark)*

Sport

3 Holiday athletics

Read this advert.

Complete the sentences. Write the correct letter in each box.

Example: This activity is for people who want to have …

A	a rest.
B	**fun.**
C	a holiday.

B

Gran Fiesta de Atletismo

¿No sabes qué hacer estas vacaciones?
¿Quieres hacer ejercicio pero también buscas mucha diversión?
¡Pues esta fiesta es para ti!

Para jóvenes de entre doce y diecisiete años, este curso es ideal, no sólo para mejorar tus habilidades deportivas – especialmente las de triatlón: ciclismo, correr y natación –
también es una gran oportunidad para hacer nuevos amigos.
Si te interesa …
Ven el lunes día 3 a la cala de Mogán – zona verde.
Trae bañador, ropa deportiva y comida
(todos los refrescos están incluidos).
Precio: 15 euros el día – imprescindible autorización de padres o tutores.

(a) The festival is for …

A	all ages.
B	young children.
C	teenagers.

☐ *(1 mark)*

(c) You might improve …

A	speaking another language.
B	your time management.
C	running, cycling and swimming.

☐ *(1 mark)*

(b) You need to bring …

A	drinks.
B	appropriate clothing.
C	friends.

☐ *(1 mark)*

(d) Participation will not be possible without …

A	parental consent.
B	a sporting qualification.
C	pre-booking.

☐ *(1 mark)*

4 Sport

Listen. What sports are mentioned? Write the correct letters in the boxes.

A   B   C   D   E   F

Example: D

☐ ☐ ☐ ☐

(4 marks)

Arranging to go out

5 Saying 'No!'

Read this magazine article.

¿Sabes decir "NO"? ¿Eres bueno dando excusas?

Preguntamos a nuestros lectores qué excusas han usado para rechazar invitaciones no deseadas y aquí están algunos de los resultados de nuestra encuesta:

- La excusa más popular, con un veintitrés por ciento de los votos, es la de tener que quedarse en casa para trabajar o hacer los deberes.
- En segundo lugar está la excusa de que mis padres no me dejan. El veinte por ciento de los chicos entrevistados prefieren ésta.
- El siete por ciento suele decir que no puede salir porque tiene colegio o trabajo al día siguiente.
- El doce por ciento dice que tiene que hacer de canguro.
- El dos por ciento dice que está esperando invitados en casa.
- El uno por ciento usa la excusa de estar malo.
- Para un diez por ciento, lo más fácil es decir que quieren ver algo guay como una peli en casa.
- A un valiente siete por ciento no le importa decir simplemente que no le apetece.
- ¡Y el uno por ciento de los entrevistados todavía usa la excusa de que tiene que lavarse el pelo!

Answer the questions **in English**.

(a) What did the magazine show in the results of its opinion poll?

.... *(1 mark)*

(b) What was the second most popular excuse?

.... *(1 mark)*

(c) What percentage of interviewees used the excuse of babysitting?

.... *(1 mark)*

(d) What is the least likely excuse given? Why?

.... *(1 mark)*

6 Going out

Conchi and Juan discuss going out. Listen to their discussion. For each topic, write **A** (if they agree), **D** (if they disagree) or **ND** (if the topic isn't discussed) in each box.

Example: the day   A

1 what time   ☐   *(1 mark)*

2 the transport   ☐   *(1 mark)*

3 the activity   ☐   *(1 mark)*

4 the meeting place   ☐   *(1 mark)*

Last weekend

7 Last weekend

Read what these young people say about last weekend.

> **David:** Pasé unos días muy agradables. El sábado por la mañana fui de compras y después, antes de ir a la fiesta de mi primo Antonio, hice mis deberes. El domingo me quedé en la cama hasta el mediodía y después salí a cenar con mis amigos.
>
> **Luci:** Mi fin de semana no fue nada interesante. Mis padres nunca me permiten salir por la noche. ¡Es una pena! Me quedé en casa. Navegué por Internet, leí y me aburrí como siempre.
>
> **Javier:** Siempre hay algo que hacer los fines de semana. El viernes, por ejemplo, fui al polideportivo y el sábado di un paseo por el campo. Desafortunadamente, el domingo tuve que ordenar mi habitación.

Who says what? Write **D** (David), **L** (Luci) or **J** (Javier) in each box.

Example: I stayed home all weekend.   L

(a) I did some housework.   ☐   *(1 mark)*   **(c)** I read a book.   ☐   *(1 mark)*

(b) I went to a restaurant.   ☐   *(1 mark)*   **(d)** I spent time with relatives.   ☐   *(1 mark)*

8 Pedro's weekend

Write the correct letter in each box.

Example: What did Pedro do on Friday evening?

A   B   C

A

(a) Where did Pedro go on Saturday morning?   **(c)** How did he feel on Saturday morning?

A   B   C   A   B   C

☐ *(1 mark)*   ☐ *(1 mark)*

(b) Who did he go with?   **(d)** What did he do on Sunday?

A   B   C   A   B   C

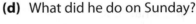

☐ *(1 mark)*   ☐ *(1 mark)*

TV programmes

9 Television

What can you watch? Write the correct letter in each box.

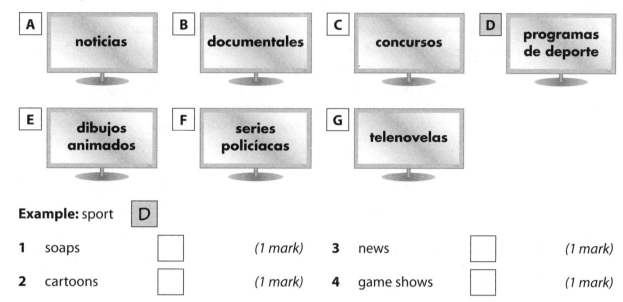

A noticias

B documentales

C concursos

D programas de deporte

E dibujos animados

F series policíacas

G telenovelas

Example: sport   D

| 1 | soaps | ☐ | *(1 mark)* | 3 | news | ☐ | *(1 mark)* |
| 2 | cartoons | ☐ | *(1 mark)* | 4 | game shows | ☐ | *(1 mark)* |

10 Marisa's favourite programmes

Listen to Marisa talking about television programmes.

> This type of question suggests she will give her opinion, so be prepared as this could be positive or negative.

(a) What does Marisa say about sports programmes?

.... *(1 mark)*

(b) What does Marisa prefer to watch?

.... *(1 mark)*

(c) What type of programmes does Marisa hate?

.... *(1 mark)*

(d) Why doesn't she like soaps?

.... *(1 mark)*

(e) Which programme does she watch every evening?

.... *(1 mark)*

(f) Why?

.... *(1 mark)*

> Take care to listen carefully for reasons. Don't just assume they are going to be the sort of reasons you might have. Listen carefully and keep an open mind!

Cinema

11 A trip to the cinema

Read about Josefina's trip to the cinema.

> El sábado pasado fui al cine con mi novio, Esteban. Vimos la película *Grito en la oscuridad*, una película estadounidense de terror.
>
> Cuenta una historia real y muy curiosa. Trata de un profesor japonés que se muda a una casa nueva. Nada más llegar, empiezan a pasar cosas extrañas y resulta que es porque hay un fantasma. Mucho antes habían asesinado allí a una joven. No te cuento cómo termina, pero es una película emocionante y misteriosa. Te la recomiendo.
>
> Josefina

Find the **four** statements which are true. Write the correct letters in the boxes.

A	Josefina went to the cinema last Saturday.
B	Josefina went to the cinema with her boyfriend.
C	Josefina saw a Canadian film.
D	The film was based on a true story.
E	Josefina thought the story was funny.

F	Josefina found the teacher unusual.
G	One of the main characters moves house.
H	The story was ten years old.
I	Josefina thought the film was exciting.

Example: A

☐ ☐ ☐ ☐   *(4 marks)*

12 An interview with Antonio Banderas

Listen to the description of an interview with Antonio Banderas. Complete the sentences. Write the correct letter in each box.

(a) Banderas didn't fulfill his dream of becoming a professional footballer because he …

A	wanted to be an actor.
B	broke his leg.
C	wasn't good enough.

☐ *(1 mark)*

(b) He was surprised at his success because …

A	Spanish actors don't do well abroad.
B	Americans don't like him.
C	he speaks English with a strong accent.

☐ *(1 mark)*

(c) The type of character he most likes to play is …

A	manipulative.
B	bad.
C	romantic.

☐ *(1 mark)*

(d) He feels unsettled because he …

A	lives in two countries.
B	hates flying.
C	never goes back to Spain.

☐ *(1 mark)*

Music

13 A music blog

Read this blog on music.

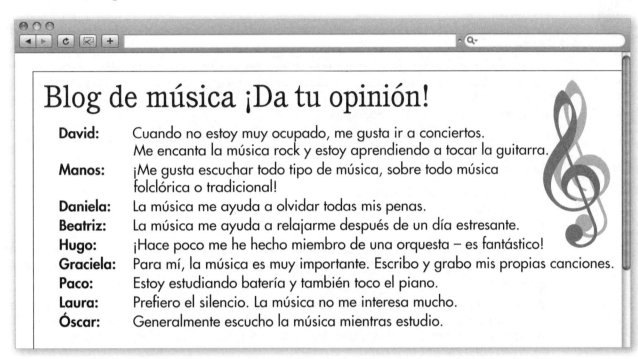

Blog de música ¡Da tu opinión!

David: Cuando no estoy muy ocupado, me gusta ir a conciertos.
Me encanta la música rock y estoy aprendiendo a tocar la guitarra.

Manos: ¡Me gusta escuchar todo tipo de música, sobre todo música folclórica o tradicional!

Daniela: La música me ayuda a olvidar todas mis penas.

Beatriz: La música me ayuda a relajarme después de un día estresante.

Hugo: ¡Hace poco me he hecho miembro de una orquesta – es fantástico!

Graciela: Para mí, la música es muy importante. Escribo y grabo mis propias canciones.

Paco: Estoy estudiando batería y también toco el piano.

Laura: Prefiero el silencio. La música no me interesa mucho.

Óscar: Generalmente escucho la música mientras estudio.

Who says the following? Write the correct name next to each statement.

Example: Music is important to me. ....._Graciela_..................................

(a) I listen to a variety of music. .... *(1 mark)*

(b) I record my own songs. .... *(1 mark)*

(c) I have music lessons. .... *(1 mark)*

(d) Music helps me to relax. .... *(1 mark)*

14 Juan Zelada – Musician

Listen to someone talking about an interview with Juan Zelada. Answer the questions below in English.

(a) Why did Juan Zelada leave Spain? .... *(1 mark)*

(b) What does he now think about …

    (i) breakfast? .... *(1 mark)*

    (ii) his musical career? .... *(1 mark)*

(c) What does he usually do …

    (i) in the mornings? .... *(1 mark)*

    (ii) in the evenings? .... *(1 mark)*

(d) Why does he say he doesn't sleep? .... *(1 mark)*

(e) What does he do once every week? .... *(1 mark)*

(f) What does he do on the radio? .... *(1 mark)*

New technology

15 An evening on the internet

Read this blog about free time and the internet.

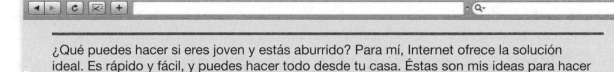

¿Qué puedes hacer si eres joven y estás aburrido? Para mí, Internet ofrece la solución ideal. Es rápido y fácil, y puedes hacer todo desde tu casa. Éstas son mis ideas para hacer actividades seguras con el ordenador:

Para empezar, están las películas. Los fines de semana solía ir mucho al cine, pero ahora descargo películas de Internet y no salgo de casa. Es más barato y además se pueden leer las opiniones de los que las han visto antes de escoger una.

Algunos padres creen que los videojuegos son una pérdida de tiempo, pero no es verdad. Jugar puede ser no sólo divertido, sino también educativo. Algunos videojuegos te hacen pensar mucho.

Otra ventaja es poder ver las noticias. Incluso los jóvenes necesitamos saber lo que pasa en el mundo. Hay muchas páginas web con noticias al minuto e información interesante sobre gente famosa.

Me gusta usar Internet para chatear con mis amigos, pero ofrece muchas más posibilidades. Por ejemplo, hace poco he empezado a estudiar francés y a aprender a tocar la guitarra. Si te apetece compartir tus fotos, puedes subirlas a Facebook. ¡Además, a todas mis amigas les gusta comprar por Internet!

Marta

In higher level reading tasks where texts are longer:
- Read the text through quickly first.
- Then read through the questions – they should give you clues as to what the text is about.
- Then read the text in more detail before you start to answer the questions properly.

Answer the following questions **in English**.

(a) What does Marta ask you at the start of her blog?

.... *(1 mark)*

(b) Mention **two** things she says that describe her views on the internet.

....

.... *(2 marks)*

(c) What are the advantages of downloading films from the internet? Mention **two**.

....

.... *(2 marks)*

(d) Why does Marta think using the internet to access the news is important?

.... *(1 mark)*

(e) Apart from contacting friends, what else does Marta use the internet for? Mention **two** things.

....

.... *(2 marks)*

Internet language

16 Internet

Read the following article.

¡Abuela a tope con Internet!

Cada tarde la abuelita doña Ángeles se mete en Internet. Descarga vídeos y juegos de todas partes del mundo. Pasa unas cuatro horas mandando y recibiendo correos electrónicos. Ángeles escribe bien con el teclado y hasta tiene su propia página web. A su marido no le gusta tanto Internet. Dice que es demasiado complicado.

Answer the following questions **in English**.

(a) When does Ángeles use the computer?

.... *(1 mark)*

(b) How long does she usually spend on the computer?

.... *(1 mark)*

(c) What does she now have?

.... *(1 mark)*

(d) Why doesn't her husband like the internet?

.... *(1 mark)*

17 Technology

Listen to Ana and Daniel discussing the internet. What is their opinion?

Write **P** (positive), **N** (negative) or **P/N** (both positive and negative) in each space in the grid.

		Daniel	Ana	
(a)	chat rooms			*(2 marks)*
(b)	web pages			*(2 marks)*
(c)	the internet in general			*(2 marks)*

Listen carefully in this type of question. The people may start by giving a positive opinion, but then go on to give a negative one. Listen carefully right to the end, to make sure.

Had a go ☐   Nearly there ☐   Nailed it! ☐

Internet pros and cons

18 Internet pros and cons

Read this article.

> Nuestro profesor invitó al colegio a una experta en informática para aconsejarnos sobre la seguridad en Internet. Todos tuvimos la oportunidad de trabajar con ella repasando nuestros blogs y considerando su contenido.
>
> Lo que más me gustó fue que empezó diciéndonos que reconocía que Internet es un medio de comunicación maravilloso y que es buenísimo para hablar con la familia y los amigos, comprar y vender en línea, y muchas otras actividades.
>
> Me di cuenta inmediatamente de que había incluido en mis blogs mucha información personal que comprometía mi privacidad y que me exponía al peligro. La experta también me explicó que había cometido un grave error al enseñar el nombre del cole en mi blog sobre los deberes. Así cualquiera podría saber dónde estoy a través del cole y de la ciudad en la que está. Para alguien malvado, sería fácil buscar nuestro colegio en Internet. Esa persona podría entonces encontrar mi barrio, y a mí.
>
> Otras pistas personales que dejé incluyen el nombre y la dirección del parque que frecuento cada día para quedar con mis amigos. Ahora entiendo cómo eso podría ayudar a alguien a encontrarme.
>
> La última y mayor equivocación fue poner una foto mía reciente que muestra claramente mi edad. Ahora tengo mucho más cuidado. He mirado y he cambiado mucha información en mi página web y escribo con más precaución cuando hablo online.
>
> Esme

> Make sure you are familiar with **verb endings**. These will help you understand the context and content of trickier passages. This text makes good use of the preterite, e.g. *invitó*, and the imperfect, e.g. *comprometía*. See if you can identify all the preterite and imperfect verbs (imperfect often ends in *–ía*).

Answer the questions **in English**.

(a) Why was an expert invited to the school?

.... *(1 mark)*

(b) What did the expert do?.. *(1 mark)*

(c) What does the expert say is good about the Internet? Name **two** things.

....

.... *(2 marks)*

(d) Why was Esme at risk ?

.... *(1 mark)*

(e) What mistake did Esme make when writing about homework?

.... *(1 mark)*

(f) What other information did Esme include that would make it easy for someone to find her?

Give **two** details.. *(2 marks)*

(g) What **two** changes has Esme made to ensure she is safer online?

....

.... *(2 marks)*

Shops

19 Town centres

Read this article about shopping.

¡Caen como moscas!

Una preocupación del gobierno actual es la progresiva desaparición en algunos lugares de España de los centros de comercio históricos dentro de las ciudades. Pero ¿cuáles son las razones? En realidad, hay muchas.

El aumento de las compras por Internet hace la vida muy difícil para los pequeños negocios y tiendas. Además de unas ganancias más reducidas, los dueños tienen que pagar el alquiler de sus locales y así les es muy difícil competir con las empresas que venden por Internet.

Los clientes están cada vez menos dispuestos a pagar los aparcamientos, que son bastante caros. Prefieren comprar desde sus hogares. Es más cómodo y, sobre todo, resulta más barato.

Con la intención de cambiar esta tendencia, el gobierno ha anunciado una serie de medidas diseñadas para revitalizar el comercio de los centros históricos de las ciudades.

En primer lugar, están haciendo una encuesta a todos los habitantes para averiguar lo que piensan que es necesario.

En segundo lugar, están organizando transporte gratis desde los aparcamientos en las afueras de la ciudad hasta los centros de comercio históricos, así la gente podrá aparcar y no sufrirá la congestión del tráfico.

Por último, van a poner más policías de servicio para reducir el nivel de delincuencia.

Si quiere más información o está interesado en saber cómo ayudar, contacte con nuestro centro de información llamando al 00 76 39 20 20.

Lo que está claro es que si no hacemos algo ahora, los centros de comercio de nuestras ciudades van a desaparecer para siempre.

Answer the questions in English.

(a) According to the article, why are town centres dying? Give **two** details.

.... *(2 marks)*

(b) Why is online shopping so popular these days? Give **two** reasons.

.... *(2 marks)*

(c) What is the government proposing to improve town-centre shopping? Give **two** details.

.... *(2 marks)*

(d) What should you do if you are interested in these projects?

.... *(1 mark)*

(e) What will happen if we don't take action?

.... *(1 mark)*

Shopping for food

20 At the supermarket

Read the shopping list.

A	huevos
B	queso
C	pescado
D	mermelada
E	champiñones
F	pan

Write the correct letter in each box.

1 cheese ☐ *(1 mark)*

2 fish ☐ *(1 mark)*

3 bread ☐ *(1 mark)*

4 eggs ☐ *(1 mark)*

21 A shopping list

Susanna is going shopping. What does she need?

A	a loaf of bread
B	250 grams of cheese
C	a dozen eggs
D	four bananas
E	a kilo of tomatoes
F	a large packet of sweets
G	2 bottles of milk
H	a large box of biscuits
I	a tin of sardines
J	a small chicken

Food words in Spanish are often similar to English words but make sure you know how they are said, as they can sound quite different in Spanish.

Listen and write the **four** correct letters in the boxes.

Example: A

☐ ☐ ☐ ☐   *(4 marks)*

At the market

22 Buying fruit and vegetables

What item does each person buy?

 A

 B

 C

 D

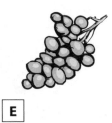 E

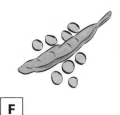 F

 G

 H

Write the correct letter in each box.

(a) Mi abuelo quiere una lechuga. ☐ *(1 mark)*

(b) A Nuria le encantarían unas uvas. ☐ *(1 mark)*

(c) Para Conchi, como siempre, zanahorias. ☐ *(1 mark)*

(d) Por último, unos guisantes para mi hermano. ☐ *(1 mark)*

23 At the market

What do they buy? Listen and write the correct item for each person **in English**.

> salad   bananas   vegetables   beans   meat
>
> apples   strawberries   melon   peaches

Example: Sebastián ..... *melon* ....

1 Begoña .... *(1 mark)*

2 Pedro .... *(1 mark)*

3 Rodrigo .... *(1 mark)*

4 Lucía .... *(1 mark)*

Clothes and colours

 B
READING

24 Buying clothes

Who says what? Write the correct name on each line.

Me encanta la moda. Trabajo en una tienda de ropa que vende cosas fabulosas. Tengo un descuento y me voy a comprar unas botas negras preciosas que tenemos en este momento.
Patri

Me gusta la moda, pero prefiero no gastar mucho dinero en ropa, así que a menudo compro en tiendas de segunda mano. Me he comprado esta chaqueta roja de cuero en una de ellas. ¡Es genial!
Paco

Me llevo estos vaqueros azules. Son americanos y muy originales. ¡Me encanta ser diferente, así que compro mi ropa cuando me voy al extranjero!
Marina

No soy aficionado a la ropa ni a la moda. Prefiero la ropa cómoda, como la de deporte. Los chándales y las zapatillas blancas son lo que más me pongo.
Juan

Example: I like sportswear. ......Juan...

(a) I buy second hand clothes. .... *(1 mark)*

(b) I buy my clothes abroad. .... *(1 mark)*

(c) I have no interest in fashion. .... *(1 mark)*

(d) I buy discounted items. .... *(1 mark)*

 G
LISTENING
 26

25 What do they want?

Listen. What do these people want to buy? Write the correct letter in each box.

A   B   C   D   E   F

Example: D

1 ☐ *(1 mark)*   2 ☐ *(1 mark)*   3 ☐ *(1 mark)*   4 ☐ *(1 mark)*

Shopping for clothes

26 The clothes party

What does Julia think? Write **P** (positive), **N** (negative) or **P/N** (both positive and negative) in each space in the grid.

○○○

🚫 Borrar   ↩ Responder   ↩ Responder a todas   ➡ Adelante   🖨 Imprimir

¡Hola, Sofía!

Anoche fui a la fiesta de ropa en casa de Ángela. Me gustó porque estaba entre amigas.

Vimos la ropa y había mucha variedad de artículos, pero los precios eran un poco caros. La ropa estaba bien hecha y además, estaba hecha con tela ecológica.

Desafortunadamente, era muy difícil probarse cosas aunque había muchos espejos.

Vale la pena ir, ¡te gustará!

Besos,

Julia

> This text is quite short so you will need to understand most of the words in order to get the right answers.

Party aspect		Opinion
Example: the venue		P
1	the variety available		*(1 mark)*
2	the quality		*(1 mark)*
3	the prices		*(1 mark)*
4	the changing facilities		*(1 mark)*

27 A dress for the prom

Part A	Part B
Listen to the first part of the recording. Which **two** statements about the dress Ángela chooses are true? Write the correct letters in the boxes. **(a)** Ángela is looking for a blue dress. **(b)** Her friend suggests she tries on one with short sleeves. **(c)** The dress Ángela prefers has a belt. **(d)** The dress with the belt is too short. ☐ ☐ *(2 marks)*	Listen to the second part of the recording. Which **two** statements are true? Write the correct letters in the boxes. **(a)** Ángela thinks the small dress is too expensive. **(b)** The small dress fits Ángela. **(c)** Ángela already has a bag to match the small dress. **(d)** Ángela chooses a longer dress of the same colour. ☐ ☐ *(2 marks)*

Returning items

28 Returns

Who says what?

No me gusta.
Mario

Está roto.
Daniela

Es demasiado grande.
David

No funciona.
Julieta

No es mi talla.
Paquito

Write the correct name on each line.

Example: I don't like it. .....Mario.................................

(a) It is the wrong size. .... *(1 mark)*

(b) It is too big. .... *(1 mark)*

(c) It is broken. .... *(1 mark)*

(d) It doesn't work. .... *(1 mark)*

29 A problem at the shop

Listen to Susana returning an item. Answer the questions **in English**.

(a) Why is Susana returning the trousers?

.... *(1 mark)*

(b) What does the assistant suggest?

.... *(1 mark)*

(c) What does the assistant ask for?

.... *(1 mark)*

(d) Where is it?

.... *(1 mark)*

(e) Why did Susana buy the trousers?

.... *(1 mark)*

> You don't need to answer in full sentences, just short notes. However, make sure you answer **in English**, as asked.

Shopping opinions

30 Shopping trends

Read what these people say about shopping.

> Me encanta ir de compras.

María

> Normalmente compro en las tiendas de uno de los centros comerciales que hay en Burgos. Me encanta la variedad y suelen ser más baratos. ¡Es la mejor manera de comprar! De vez en cuando compro por Internet también.

Pepito

> Yo no soy aficionada a comprar. Sin embargo, me gusta ir a la moda. Últimamente muchos de mis amigos hacen fiestas para vender ropa y maquillaje y me gusta eso. ¡Ganan dinero también!

Antonia

> No entiendo por qué a la gente le gusta ir de compras. Odio hacer colas. Yo prefiero quedarme en casa y comprar por correo.

Elvira

> Siempre compro cositas en la tienda que está al lado de mi casa porque es más práctico.

Julián

How do these people describe their shopping experiences? Write **P** (positive), **N** (negative) or **P + N** (both positive and negative) in each box.

Example: María: ☐ P

1	Antonia	☐	*(1 mark)*	**3**	Pepito	☐ *(1 mark)*
2	Elvira	☐	*(1 mark)*	**4**	Julián	☐ *(1 mark)*

31 Shopping preferences

Who says what? Listen and write the correct name on each line.

Example: I love shopping. ...*Pablo*...

(a) I quite like large shopping centres. .... *(1 mark)*

(b) I don't like local shops. .... *(1 mark)*

(c) I prefer window shopping. .... *(1 mark)*

(d) I like to shop from catalogues. .... *(1 mark)*

Ana	Pablo	Inés

Pocket money

32 Spending pocket money

Read this article about pocket money.

> # ¡A gastar! ¿En qué gastan su dinero los chicos de hoy en día?
>
> Varía bastante en qué gastan los jóvenes su paga, pero lo cierto es que ha cambiado mucho. Hoy en día parece ser que no sólo compran cosas como ropa, revistas y maquillaje – ahora las cosas más populares son los cafés en Starbucks, comidas en restaurantes, saldo para el móvil y alcohol.
>
> Lo más sorprendente es que incluso hay otros jóvenes que usan su dinero para crear nuevos proyectos. Va creciendo la cantidad de chicos que tienen sus propios negocios. ¡Tenemos una generación de empresarios*!
>
> Sin embargo, algo que no ha cambiado nada es que los jóvenes quieren ser adultos y copian lo que ven hacer a los mayores.

According to the article, which **four** statements are correct?

*empresario = entrepreneur

A	The things young people spend their money on has changed a lot.
B	Young people have less money than they used to.
C	Young people spend money on magazines.
D	Food and drink are popular buys now.
E	No one buys clothes and make-up any more.
F	The number of young people involved in businesses is on the increase.
G	Young people don't worry about money at all.
H	Young people still want to appear older.
I	Young people don't want to rely on their parents for money.

Write the **four** correct letters in the box.

Example: C

☐ ☐ ☐ ☐ (4 marks)

33 Opinions on pocket money

Listen to these young people discussing whether parents should give children pocket money. What is their opinion?

Write **P** (positive), **N** (negative) or **P + N** (both positive and negative) in each box.

Example: Julia N

1   Mario ☐ (1 mark)   3   Merce ☐ (1 mark)

2   Adriana ☐ (1 mark)   4   Joaquín ☐ (1 mark)

Holiday destinations

34 Favourite destinations

Where do these people like to go on holiday?

Marta	A mí me gusta la ciudad.
Enrique	A mí me gusta la playa porque soy muy deportista.
Luisa	Me encanta viajar y, si es posible, al extranjero.
Manuel	Lo que necesito es relajarme y para eso, el campo siempre me parece la mejor opción.
Clara	Como me encanta esquiar, prefiero ir a la montaña.

Write the correct name on each line.

Example: cities ..... Marta ....

1 countryside .... *(1 mark)*

2 beach .... *(1 mark)*

3 abroad .... *(1 mark)*

4 mountains .... *(1 mark)*

35 Holiday destinations

Where do they go on holiday? Listen and write the correct letter in each box.

A   B   C

E   F   G

Example: B

1 ☐ *(1 mark)*   **3** ☐ *(1 mark)*

2 ☐ *(1 mark)*   **4** ☐ *(1 mark)*

Holiday accommodation

36 Where to stay

Read what these people say about holiday accommodation.

Roberto	Me encanta quedarme en hoteles. Me gusta no tener que hacer mi cama ni ayudar en nada. Allí hay gente que te lo hace todo. ¡Es genial!
Pablo	Me gusta estar al aire libre – en un camping, por ejemplo – y hacer diferentes actividades. Soy una persona sencilla y no necesito muchos lujos.
Maruja	Lo que a mí me gusta es poder hacer mis deportes preferidos – tengo un kayak y me gusta nadar largas distancias. Es muy difícil practicarlos en la ciudad donde vivo. Por el camino me alojo en albergues juveniles.
Juli	No soy aficionado a las vacaciones en hoteles. Prefiero pasar mis vacaciones en casa de familiares y amigos.

Choose the correct person. Write **R** (Roberto), **P** (Pablo), **M** (Maruja) or **J** (Juli) in each box.

Example: Who likes hotels?　　R

(a) Who stays in youth hostels?　　　　　　　　　　☐　　*(1 mark)*

(b) Who doesn't like to be indoors?　　　　　　　　☐　　*(1 mark)*

(c) Who doesn't like work?　　　　　　　　　　　　☐　　*(1 mark)*

(d) Who cares more about who to spend a holiday with?　☐　*(1 mark)*

37 Holiday accommodation

Where do these people stay? Listen and write the correct letter in each box.

A	cousin's house
B	hotel
C	city flat
D	tent
E	caravan
F	youth hostel

> Read the options A–F before you listen and try to think of the Spanish vocabulary you will hear.

Example: Marcelo　　C

1　Paulina　　☐　　*(1 mark)*

2　Rogelio　　☐　　*(1 mark)*

3　Samuel　　☐　　*(1 mark)*

4　Eva　　☐　　*(1 mark)*

Booking accommodation

38 Booking a hotel room

Estimado señor:

El año pasado pasamos una semana maravillosa en su hotel. Como sé que se llena rápidamente en temporada alta, le escribo para solicitar una reserva para quince días desde el 21 de julio. Queremos una habitación doble con baño y balcón, y otra sencilla con vistas al mar.

¿Nos podría ofrecer unas habitaciones más cerca de la piscina este año? Está cerca de todas las demás cosas y podríamos vigilar a los niños sin tener que bañarnos todo el rato.

Como vamos en coche, también necesitamos reservar una plaza de aparcamiento ¿Costaría más? Y además pensamos llevar al perro. ¿Sería eso posible?

Y una preguntita más: ¿cuánto costaría el alojamiento con media pensión?

Gracias por su ayuda.

Le saluda atentamente,

Gregorio Ferrer

> Be sure to include all details so as to get maximum marks in a question like this – so talk about each room and what they want in it.

Answer the questions **in English**.

(a) Why are these tourists returning to the hotel?

.... *(1 mark)*

(b) What accommodation do they want? Mention **two** things.

.... *(2 marks)*

(c) (i) Where do they want the rooms to be?

.... *(1 mark)*

(ii) Why? Give **two** reasons.

....

.... *(2 marks)*

(d) What do they ask about parking?

.... *(1 mark)*

(e) What else do they ask? Name **two** things.

....

.... *(2 marks)*

Staying in a hotel

39 Hotel search

Read what these people say about staying in hotels.

Marcelo:	Nuestra habitación tiene que estar limpia y ser cómoda. Si no, no me lo pasaré bien.
Benjamín:	Quiero un hotel tranquilo con vistas al mar. Quiero poder dormir por la noche sin ruidos.
Sofía:	Para mí es superimportante que la comida sea buena. Quiero mucha variedad y quiero pensión completa.
Fátima:	El hotel tiene que tener piscina, sala de juegos y conexión a Internet. Supongo que tiene que ser de cuatro estrellas.
Yulen:	La verdad es que el hotel no puede ser muy caro.

Who mentions what? Write the correct name on each line.

Example: cleanliness ..... _Marcelo_ ....

(a) cost .... *(1 mark)*

(b) food .... *(1 mark)*

(c) sleep quality .... *(1 mark)*

(d) facilities .... *(1 mark)*

40 Hotel choices

What do they say? Listen and write the correct letter in each box.

A	I always book full board.
B	I have to have a balcony.
C	I am only interested in a sea view.
D	I prefer a room with a shower.
E	I don't need a half board deal.
F	I like to make a reservation for a fortnight.
G	I only stay in hotels with a sea view.

Example: **B**

1   Claudia   ☐   *(1 mark)*

2   Francisco   ☐   *(1 mark)*

3   Nuria   ☐   *(1 mark)*

4   Nacho   ☐   *(1 mark)*

Staying on a campsite

41 Camping

Read this e-mail from Federico.

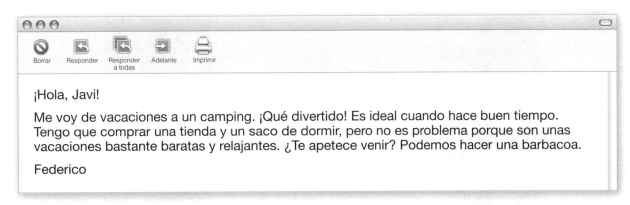

¡Hola, Javi!

Me voy de vacaciones a un camping. ¡Qué divertido! Es ideal cuando hace buen tiempo. Tengo que comprar una tienda y un saco de dormir, pero no es problema porque son unas vacaciones bastante baratas y relajantes. ¿Te apetece venir? Podemos hacer una barbacoa.

Federico

According to the e-mail, which **four** of the following statements are true?

A	Javi is planning a camping holiday.
B	Camping is very popular.
C	Camping is best in good weather.
D	Camping is very uncomfortable.

E	You need transport to go camping.
F	You need to buy the right equipment.
G	Camping is relaxing.
H	Federico thinks Javi should come too.

Write the correct letters in the boxes.

☐ ☐ ☐ ☐

(4 marks)

42 A camping trip

Listen to what Ana says about her camping trip. Complete the sentences by writing the correct letter in each box.

Example: Ana said her stay was …

A	good.
B	OK.
C	terrible.

A

This passage will be in the past, so make sure you revise the different forms of the past.

(a) The facilities were …

A	excellent.
B	appalling.
C	acceptable.

☐ *(1 mark)*

(c) The beds were …

A	inflatable.
B	soft.
C	hard.

☐ *(1 mark)*

(b) The tent was …

A	too small.
B	too big.
C	a good size.

☐ *(1 mark)*

(d) At night it was …

A	warm.
B	peaceful.
C	noisy.

☐ *(1 mark)*

Holiday activities

43 On holiday

Who likes which activity? Write the correct name on each line.

| Me gusta hacer surf. |

Mario

| Quiero comprar recuerdos. |

Felicia

| Me encanta nadar. |

Santiago

| Me encanta sacar fotos. |

Daniela

| Me gusta descansar. |

Quique

Example: swimming ..... *Santiago* ....

(a) photography .... *Daniela* .... *(1 mark)*

(b) a water sport ..... *Mario* .... *(1 mark)*

(c) shopping for souvenirs .... *(1 mark)*

(d) relaxing .... *(1 mark)*

44 A typical holiday

Complete the sentences. Listen and write the correct letter in the boxes.

Example: Carlos went on holiday with his …

A	girlfriend.
B	**family.**
C	friends.

☐ B

(a) He spent most days in the …

A	bar.
B	games room.
C	pool.

☐ *(1 mark)*

(b) In the afternoons he went …

A	cycling.
B	horse riding.
C	rollerblading.

☐ *(1 mark)*

(c) He had dinner …

A	at home.
B	in the hotel.
C	out.

☐ *(1 mark)*

(d) If the weather was bad they …

A	relaxed.
B	took photos.
C	went bowling.

☐ *(1 mark)*

Holiday preferences

45 Choosing a holiday

Who says what? Write **J** (Juan), **M** (María) or **B** (both) in each box.

> **Juan:** Yo creo que irse de vacaciones es una idea estupenda, pero preferiría ir después de mis exámenes del cole. Como ya tengo dieciséis años, preferiría pasar las vacaciones con mis amigos en vez de con mis padres, como de costumbre. Así que a partir del diez de junio estaría bien para mí porque Carlos tiene su último examen el día anterior. Es bastante difícil llegar a un acuerdo con respecto al destino porque somos seis. Todos quieren ir a Grecia, pero yo no estoy tan seguro. Creo que hará demasiado calor.
>
> **María:** No me interesa para nada irme de vacaciones con mis amigos. Dentro de tres meses cumpliré dieciocho años, pero no tengo ganas de estar lejos de mi familia, como muchos jóvenes. De hecho, pienso pasar mis vacaciones este año con mi hermana. La semana que viene vamos a ir juntas a una agencia de viajes para organizar un viaje de tres semanas a México, porque me encanta el sol. Es el momento ideal, ya que ahora, mi tío está trabajando allí. Si no aprovechamos esta oportunidad, será una pena porque en casa de mi tío no tenemos que pagar alojamiento.

Example: I'm looking forward to my holidays.   B

(a) I want to go away with friends.   ☐   *(1 mark)*

(b) I'm not sure where to go.   ☐   *(1 mark)*

(c) I like holidays in very hot countries.   ☐   *(1 mark)*

(d) I want to go abroad.   ☐   *(1 mark)*

(e) I'm worried about the cost.   ☐   *(1 mark)*

(f) I'm travelling in a big group.   ☐   *(1 mark)*

(g) I'm ready to book my trip.   ☐   *(1 mark)*

(h) School commitments mean I can't go on holiday right now.   ☐   *(1 mark)*

46 A holiday in Andalucía

Listen to Lucía, David and Nacho discussing holiday options. What do they think about the holiday in Andalucía?

Write **P** (positive), **N** (negative) or **P/N** (both positive and negative) for each person in the boxes.

1   Lucía   ☐   *(1 mark)*

2   David   ☐   *(1 mark)*

3   Nacho   ☐   *(1 mark)*

Future holiday plans

47 A planned holiday

Read what Nuria plans to do during her holiday.

Sábado:
Ya he quedado con mis amigos para pasar el día relajándonos tomando el sol en la playa y jugando en la arena. Tengo muchas ganas de tomar un helado y pasar un rato con un buen libro.

Domingo:
Iré a misa en la iglesia antigua y después iré al bosque y montaré a caballo por los alrededores, que son muy bonitos. Estoy deseando estar al aire libre.

Lunes:
No puedo pasar las vacaciones sin visitar el famoso lago para hacer vela y natación. Será el lugar ideal para disfrutar del campo. También daré una vuelta en bicicleta.

Martes:
Como quiero aprender a cocinar comida típica casera, he reservado una plaza en el curso de cocina del gran hotel Félix. Sé que volveré a casa sabiendo preparar unos platos estupendos.

Miércoles:
Pasaré la mayor parte del día haciendo yoga o clases de baile. Tendré que pasar la tarde haciendo la maleta para el viaje de vuelta.

Jueves:
¡No quiero ni pensarlo! Todo se habrá terminado y estaré rumbo a casa. ¡Qué pena!

Which activity takes place on each day?

	Planned activity
A	packing
B	doing watersports
C	working out
D	spending time at the beach
E	sightseeing and outdoor activities

F	travelling
G	learning a new skill
H	reading
I	going rock climbing

> When you see categories like 'watersports' think of all the vocabulary you know which could come under this heading, and then search for it in the text.

Write the correct letter in each box.

(a) Sunday ☐ *(1 mark)*   **(b)** Monday ☐ *(1 mark)*   **(c)** Tuesday ☐ *(1 mark)*

(d) Wednesday ☐ *(1 mark)*   **(e)** Thursday ☐ *(1 mark)*

48 Next summer

Listen to Inés talking about her holiday plans.

A	sailing	D	eating	G	climbing
B	walking	E	riding	H	sightseeing
C	cycling	F	resting	I	swimming

Complete the sentences. Write the correct letter in each box.

1 In Marbella she hopes she will be ☐. *(1 mark)*

2 In the mornings she will go ☐. *(1 mark)*

3 She will spend the afternoons ☐. *(1 mark)*

4 Inés plans to spend the evenings ☐. *(1 mark)*

Holiday experiences

49 My summer holiday

Read this e-mail from Guillermo.

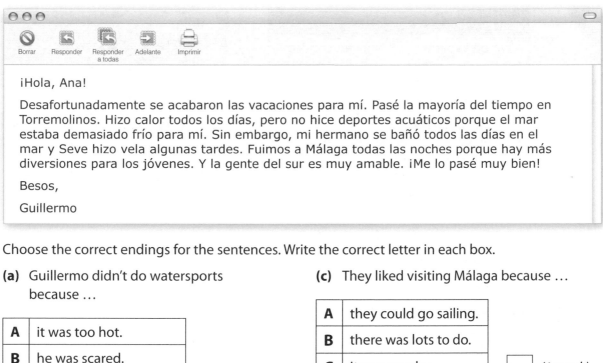

Borrar   Responder   Responder a todas   Adelante   Imprimir

¡Hola, Ana!

Desafortunadamente se acabaron las vacaciones para mí. Pasé la mayoría del tiempo en Torremolinos. Hizo calor todos los días, pero no hice deportes acuáticos porque el mar estaba demasiado frío para mí. Sin embargo, mi hermano se bañó todos las días en el mar y Seve hizo vela algunas tardes. Fuimos a Málaga todas las noches porque hay más diversiones para los jóvenes. Y la gente del sur es muy amable. ¡Me lo pasé muy bien!

Besos,

Guillermo

Choose the correct endings for the sentences. Write the correct letter in each box.

(a) Guillermo didn't do watersports because …

A	it was too hot.
B	he was scared.
C	the water was too cold.

☐ *(1 mark)*

(b) Guillermo's brother went swimming …

A	several times.
B	every day.
C	if it wasn't too cold.

☐ *(1 mark)*

(c) They liked visiting Málaga because …

A	they could go sailing.
B	there was lots to do.
C	it was nearby.

☐ *(1 mark)*

(d) Guillermo finds the people in that area …

A	very kind.
B	very rude.
C	very interesting.

☐ *(1 mark)*

50 Holiday memories

Listen to Raquel remembering a special holiday. Answer the questions **in English**.

(a) Where did her grandmother live?

.... *(1 mark)*

(b) Who did she meet there?

.... *(1 mark)*

(c) What did they do on a special day she describes? Mention **two** things.

....

.... *(2 marks)*

(d) What did she do with her brothers?

.... *(1 mark)*

(e) Why didn't they go back?

.... *(1 mark)*

Countries and nationalities

1   Which country?

Where do these people come from?

Stacey:
Vivo en España, pero nací en Londres.

Julie:
Me gusta ser galesa.

David:
Soy de Escocia, pero no me considero británico.

Jim:
Soy estadounidense. ¡Qué fantástico!

Stefan:
Estoy orgulloso de ser alemán.

Write the correct name on each line.

Example: Germany ....Stefan................................

(a)   Wales ....   *(1 mark)*

(b)   Scotland ....   *(1 mark)*

(c)   England ....   *(1 mark)*

(d)   United States ....   *(1 mark)*

2   My roots

Listen to these people talking about where they come from. Match each one with the appropriate ID by writing the correct letter in each box.

A
Father: Irish
Mother: French
Lives in: France

B
Father: American
Mother: Spanish
Lives in: Spain

C
Father: American
Mother: American
Lives in: USA

D
Father: French
Mother: Spanish
Lives in: Wales

E
Father: German
Mother: Greek
Lives in: Portugal

F
Father: Spanish
Mother: English
Lives in: England

G
Father: Spanish
Mother: English
Lives in: Scotland

Example: A

1   ☐   *(1 mark)*   3   ☐   *(1 mark)*   5   ☐   *(1 mark)*

2   ☐   *(1 mark)*   4   ☐   *(1 mark)*

My house

3 A housing advert

Read this advert for a luxury house.

Gran Oferta - Casa de lujo en Torrevieja

¿Quiere vivir en una zona exclusiva y protegida?

Les ofrecemos una ganga: **Casa Dorada**

Ubicada en un pequeño pueblo valenciano, esta vivienda con encanto dispone de cinco dormitorios, cuatro baños y dos aseos.

Tiene piscina, pista de tenis y un jardín precioso con vistas espléndidas al mar. El recinto tiene un sistema de seguridad con cámaras, wi-fi, antena parabólica y múltiples televisores de pantalla plana.

Cerca de centros comerciales de lujo.

What is the property like? Write the correct letter in each box.

(a) Price

A	Too expensive
B	A good price
C	In a bad neighbourhood

B *(1 mark)*

(b) Space available

A	Room for lots of people
B	Ideal for just one person
C	It is a hotel.

  (1 mark)

(c) Sports facilities and garden

A	Great for doing sports
B	You can't swim there.
C	Has views of the mountains

  (1 mark)

(d) Facilities

A	In a dangerous area
B	Doesn't have the latest technology
C	You can watch films.

  (1 mark)

(e) Location

A	Not far from the shops
B	A few metres from the beach
C	Near some caves

  (1 mark)

4 Juan's home

Listen to what Juan says about his home. Answer the following questions **in English**.

(a) Where does Juan live? .... *(1 mark)*

(b) Describe the town. Mention **two** things. ....

.... *(2 marks)*

(c) Where is his flat? .... *(1 mark)*

(d) What rooms are in the flat? Mention **two**. .... *(2 marks)*

(e) What is the problem with living where he does? .... *(1 mark)*

Had a go ☐ Nearly there ☐ Nailed it! ☐

My room

5 Raúl and Inés

Read what Raúl and Inés say about their rooms.

Raúl

No está mal mi habitación, pero tengo que compartirla con mi hermano y preferiría tener mi propio cuarto. Es pequeña y no hay sitio suficiente para todas nuestras cosas. Necesito un armario más grande. Lo bueno es que como mi cama está al lado de la ventana, se ve el mar y eso me encanta.

Inés

Mi habitación es grande. También es la de mi hermana, Susana, y eso está bien porque no me gusta estar sola. Lo malo es que somos muy desordenadas y mi madre siempre nos regaña. Es amplia y tenemos muchos muebles. Acabamos de comprar un equipo de música nuevo, pero Susana pone la música demasiado alta.

Identify the people. Write **R** (Raúl), **I** (Inés) or **B** (both Raúl and Inés) in each box.

(a) Who shares a room? | R | *(1 mark)*

(b) Who has an untidy room? | R | *(1 mark)*

(c) Who has good views? | I | *(1 mark)*

(d) Who has a room that's too small? | R | *(1 mark)*

(e) Who likes company? | I | *(1 mark)*

(f) Who sleeps by the window? | R | *(1 mark)*

(g) Who likes music? | B | *(1 mark)*

(h) Who talks about the size of their room? | B | *(1 mark)*

6 Samuel's room

Listen to what Samuel says about his room. Which of the following statements best sums up what Samuel thinks about his room?

Write the correct letter in the box.

(a)

A	Samuel likes most things about his room.
B	Samuel likes everything about his room.
C	Samuel dislikes most things about his room.

(1 mark)

(b)

A	He bought all the furniture.
B	He bought the tables and shelves.
C	He bought the bed and wardrobe.

(1 mark)

(c)

A	He still needs to buy bookshelves.
B	He already has bookshelves.
C	He doesn't need bookshelves.

(1 mark)

(d)

A	The curtains are the wrong size.
B	The curtains are the wrong colour.
C	The curtains are the wrong material.

(1 mark)

Helping at home

7 Julia's housework

Read what Julia says about helping at home.

> Ayudo bastante en casa, no como mi hermano mayor ¡que no hace nada! Tengo mis preferencias e intento evitar lo que menos me gusta hacer. Por ejemplo, si tengo elección, quito la mesa en vez de poner el lavaplatos porque si no, el agua me estropea las manos. Siempre paso la aspiradora porque me parece que es como hacer ejercicio. Es mejor que limpiar mi habitación, que es muy aburrido. Odio cortar el césped, pero no me importa pasear al perro porque es buena compañía y es mi mejor amigo.

Answer the questions in English.

(a) Which chore does Julia say she prefers to loading the dishwasher, and why?

　(i) *Setting the table* .... *(1 mark)*

　(ii) *Walking her dog* .... *(1 mark)*

(b) What chore does she always do, and why?

　Walking her dog because he is good company .... *(2 marks)*

(c) What does she prefer to cutting the grass, and why?

　Walking her dog .... *(2 marks)*

8 Clara helps at home

Listen to what Clara says about helping at home. Choose the correct ending for each sentence and write the letter in each box.

(a) Clara …

A	doesn't see the point of helping.
B	recognises the importance of helping.
C	doesn't have an opinion.

☐ *(1 mark)*

(b) She …

A	helps every day.
B	doesn't have time to help.
C	doesn't have to help.

☐ *(1 mark)*

(c) Clara …

A	will help more in the future.
B	is leaving home.
C	doesn't intend to help in future.

☐ *(1 mark)*

(d) She …

A	only makes her bed.
B	only does the washing.
C	only tidies her room.

☐ *(1 mark)*

My neighbourhood

9 Nuria's letter

Read Nuria's letter.

> ¡Hola Raquel!
>
> ¡Cuánto tiempo! No te lo vas a creer, ¡por fin me he escapado de la ciudad!
>
> Te escribo para contarte que acabo de mudarme de casa. Ahora estamos viviendo en una casita en el campo. Está al lado de un bosque y ¡hasta hay un río al final del jardín! El fin de semana pasado fui a dar un paseo y terminé bañándome, ¡el agua estaba deliciosa!
>
> Lo bueno es que hay tanto espacio y ya sabes que me encanta el campo y en los alrededores hay una gran variedad de vegetación y animales.
>
> Antes odiaba estar en plena ciudad y tener que soportar el ruido y la contaminación que eran horribles, así que ¡es un placer estar aquí!
>
> Tienes que venir a verlo. ¿Cuándo estás libre? Me encantaría enseñártelo todo y podríamos ir de camping.
>
> Un abrazo,
>
> *Nuria*

Answer the questions **in English**.

1   (a) Why is Nuria writing the letter?

.... *(1 mark)*

(b) How does she describe where she lives? Give **two** details.

.... *(2 marks)*

(c) What does she like about where she lives? Name **two** things.

.... *(2 marks)*

(d) What disadvantages does she mention about where she was before?
Name **two** things.

.... *(2 marks)*

(e) What future event does she refer to?

.... *(1 mark)*

10 Fran's hometown

What does Fran think about where he lives? Listen and write **P** (positive), **N** (negative) or **P/N** (both positive and negative) on each line next to each thing he talks about.

(a) activities ☐   *(1 mark)*   **(d)** cars ☐   *(1 mark)*

(b) employment ☐   *(1 mark)*   **(e)** town hall attitude ☐   *(1 mark)*

(c) people ☐   *(1 mark)*

Places in town

11 Mateo's town

Part A

Read what Mateo says about his town. What places of interest does he refer to?

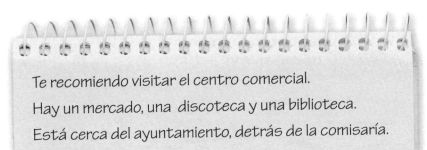

Te recomiendo visitar el centro comercial.

Hay un mercado, una discoteca y una biblioteca.

Está cerca del ayuntamiento, detrás de la comisaría.

| A | B | C | D | E |

Write the correct **three** letters in the boxes.

☐ ☐ ☐

(3 marks)

Part B

Where is the shopping centre? Write the correct **two** letters in the boxes.

A	It is close to the town hall.
B	It is 10 minutes from the post office.
C	On the corner of the high street.
D	It is behind the police station.

> Many place names are the same, or similar, in Spanish and English, Look for these words first.

☐ ☐

(2 marks)

12 Places in town

Where do these people want to go? Listen and write the correct letter in each box.

A	park	E	hairdresser's
B	theatre	F	ice rink
C	museum	G	cinema
D	library	H	swimming pool

(a) Sara ☐   *(1 mark)*   **(c)** Amina ☐   *(1 mark)*

(b) Julio ☐   *(1 mark)*   **(d)** Serena ☐   *(1 mark)*

At the tourist office

13 Signs in town

Read these signs.

A
folleto de
excursiones

B
biblioteca municipal
horario: 9:00 – 18:00

C
lista de albergues
juveniles

D
horario de
autobuses

E
museo

F
mapa de la región

G
oficina de
turismo

H
lista de
playas
bonitas

Where do these people need to look for information? Write the correct letters in the boxes.

(a) Grace wants to visit the castle. ☐ *(1 mark)*

(b) Paco needs to know when the bus leaves. ☐ *(1 mark)*

(c) Julia is looking for accommodation. ☐ *(1 mark)*

(d) Luca needs directions. ☐ *(1 mark)*

14 At the tourist office

What information do these tourists want? Listen and write the correct letter in each box.

A	train times
B	directions
C	excursions
D	accommodation
E	opening hours

1 ☐   *(1 mark)*   **2** ☐   *(1 mark)*   **3** ☐   *(1 mark)*

Things to do in town

15 Rodrigo's town

Read Rodrigo's opinions about his town. What does he say about each place?

Write **P** (positive), **N** (negative) or **P/N** (both positive and negative) in each space.

Example: Me encanta visitar edificios históricos. → P

A No me gusta ir a la catedral. ☐ *(1 mark)*

B Ver el puerto no es muy interesante. ☐ *(1 mark)*

C Practicar deporte en el parque es bueno para la salud. ☐ *(1 mark)*

D ¿Ir a la piscina? ¡No, gracias! ☐ *(1 mark)*

E Me encanta comer en restaurantes aunque es caro. ☐ *(1 mark)*

F Conocer la cultura es mi actividad preferida. ☐ *(1 mark)*

G Me gusta ir a la galería de arte, pero a veces es un poco aburrido. ☐ *(1 mark)*

H Ir al parque temático es divertido. ☐ *(1 mark)*

Watch out for negative expressions such as *no*.

16 What to do in town

Listen to these people talking about their towns.

Write the activity mentioned and the speaker's opinion **P** (positive), **N** (negative) or **P + N** (both positive and negative) in each space.

		Activity	Opinion	
Example: Roque		cinema	P	*(2 marks)*
1	Laura			*(2 marks)*
2	Feliciano			*(2 marks)*
3	Margot			*(2 marks)*
4	Seve			*(2 marks)*
5	Paula			*(2 marks)*

Had a go ☐   Nearly there ☐   Nailed it! ☐

Signs around town

17 In the car park

Look at these road signs. What do they say?

> Está prohibido aparcar delante de la entrada.

> El aparcamiento está abierto hasta el día 24 de diciembre.

> Los servicios están cerrados después de las diez de la noche.

Choose the correct **three** statements.

A	You can park anywhere.
B	The car park isn't open on Christmas Day.
C	The toilets are out of order.
D	The toilets are only open during the day.
E	You mustn't park in front of the entrance
F	The car park is open 24 hours a day.

Write the correct letters in the boxes.

☐ ☐ ☐   *(3 marks)*

18 Signs around town

Which sign is each of these people referring to?

A	**No smoking**

B	**Town centre**

C	**Car park**

D	**Entrance**

E	Cashpoint

F	**Exit**

G	**Station**

H	No dogs

Listen and fill in each space in the grid. Add the letter of the sign and the reason.

	Sign	Reason	
1			*(2 marks)*
2			*(2 marks)*
3			*(2 marks)*
4			*(2 marks)*

Where I live

C

19 What is my town like?

Read these tweets by people about life in their home towns.

> **@Carmen:**
> Me gusta mi ciudad porque la gente es generosa. Sin embargo, no hay muchas diversiones para los jóvenes. Han cerrado el cine y no hay club de jóvenes.

> **@Santi:** He vivido diez años al lado del mar. Es genial. Los fines de semana en verano son fantásticos porque hay muchos turistas y la ciudad está muy animada. Lo único malo es que en invierno todo está cerrado.

> **@Consuelo:**
> Vivo en una ciudad grande e industrial, así que hay bastante contaminación. Tiene muchas ventajas, pero desafortunadamente hay mucho paro, así que la gente sale poco. Creo que en el futuro me mudaré a otra ciudad.

Answer the questions. Write **C** (Carmen), **S** (Santi) or **L** (Lorena) in each box.

1 Who is thinking of moving away? ☐ *(1 mark)*

2 Who says their opinion depends on the season? ☐ *(1 mark)*

3 Who says there is little to do where they live? ☐ *(1 mark)*

4 Who says people don't go out much? ☐ *(1 mark)*

5 Who speaks well of the people who live in their town? ☐ *(1 mark)*

A

20 Bernardo's home town

Listen to Bernardo talking about his home town. Answer the following questions **in English**.

Part A

(a) How does Bernardo feel about where he lives? .... *(1 mark)*

(b) What does he say is good about it? .... *(1 mark)*

(c) What does he say about the people who live there? .... *(1 mark)*

(d) Name one of the disadvantages of living there. .... *(1 mark)*

Part B

(a) Where will Bernardo take his penfriend? Name **two** places. .... *(1 mark)*

(b) What is special about the place he will take him to eat? .... *(1 mark)*

(c) Why will Bernard's friend like it there? .... *(1 mark)*

Town description

21 Memories of my town

Read this article.

> Yo había tenido una infancia bastante normal y sencilla en mi pueblecito del norte de Chile, hasta el tremendo día del cinco de agosto del dos mil diez en el que hubo una tormenta enorme. Me acordaré siempre de mi tío Félix, que volvía cada día de la mina San José, donde trabajaba, y decía que un desastre estaba al caer. Y así fue. Ese día la mina se derrumbó y se quedaron atrapadas treinta y tres personas – incluyendo a mi tío. Yo estaba desesperada y pensaba que se iba a morir. Por suerte, después de sesenta y nueve días bajo tierra, salieron todos vivos, la mayoría sin heridas graves. A mi tío le tuvieron que operar los dientes, pero nada más. Estoy muy agradecida porque sobrevivió y también porque no piensa bajar a la mina nunca más. A pesar de lo difícil que es encontrar trabajo por aquí, José ha conseguido un puesto como mecánico en Copiapó. ¡Menos mal!

Answer the questions **in English**.

(a) What overall initial impression does this girl give of her childhood?

.... *(1 mark)*

(b) What did her uncle always talk about?

.... *(1 mark)*

(c) Why was he right?

.... *(1 mark)*

(d) What happened to the people?

.... *(1 mark)*

(e) What does she say about employment in her region?

.... *(1 mark)*

(f) Why is she relieved? Give **two** reasons.

    (i) .... *(1 mark)*

    (ii) .... *(1 mark)*

(g) What has happened to her uncle since?

.... *(1 mark)*

> You don't need to answer in full sentences, but do make sure your answers are clear.

Weather

22 Blogging

Read the following blog entries about the weather.

> **Título:** El clima
>
> **Antonio:** Me encanta el sol.
>
> **María:** Cuando llueve, me quedo en casa.
>
> **Jesús:** Me encanta la nieve, porque me gusta mucho esquiar.
>
> **Isabel:** Cuando hace buen tiempo se puede dar una vuelta en bici.
>
> **Martín:** Cuando hace frío no puedo salir al jardín.

Write the correct name on each line. Who is talking about …

(a) sunny weather? .... *(1 mark)*

(b) fine weather? .... *(1 mark)*

(c) rainy weather? .... *(1 mark)*

(d) cold weather? .... *(1 mark)*

(e) snowy weather? .... *(1 mark)*

23 Weather forecast

What will the weather be like in each region? Listen and make notes **in English**.

Example:

Place	Weather
Gran Canaria	....hot............ and ....sunny............

(a)

Place	Weather
Andorra	..............................and ....

(2 marks)

(c)

Place	Weather
Mexico	..............................and ....

(2 marks)

(b)

Place	Weather
Cantabria	..............................and ....

(2 marks)

(d)

Place	Weather
Argentina	..............................and ....

(2 marks)

Celebrations at home

24 Lucía's Christmas

Read Lucía's letter about her family's Christmas celebrations.

> ¡Hola, Fran!
>
> Te escribo para darte las gracias por el iPod que me mandaste por Navidad. Me encanta y llevaba todo el año deseando tener uno. Ahora puedo escuchar toda mi música favorita.
>
> ¿Qué tal tus fiestas por allí? Las mías, muy bien, pero en vez de lo tradicional, este año decidimos hacer algo diferente y la verdad que fue un gran éxito. En Nochebuena, por ejemplo, nos reunimos toda la familia, como de costumbre, para jugar y cantar, pero en vez de tomar los platos típicos navideños, llamamos a Telepizza. ¡Qué rico!
>
> Cuando vengas en Nochevieja, estamos planeando hacer una cena de gala con comida especial y nos vamos a vestir como estrellas de cine. Nos lo pasaremos de maravilla. ¿Qué te parece?
>
> ¡Hasta pronto!
>
> Lucía

What does Lucía talk about in her letter? Write the correct letter in each box.

(a) Lucia …

A	has wanted an iPod for a long time.
B	doesn't like her present.
C	already had an iPod.

☐ *(1 mark)*

(b) Lucia asks …

A	Fran about her presents.
B	if Fran has had a good time.
C	if Fran got lots of presents.

☐ *(1 mark)*

(c) On Christmas eve …

A	they celebrated as they always do.
B	they had fast food.
C	they went to church.

☐ *(1 mark)*

(d) On New Year's Eve …

A	Fran is having a party.
B	Fran is going to the cinema.
C	Fran is coming to Lucía's.

☐ *(1 mark)*

25 A birthday celebration

Listen to Cecilia talking about her birthday celebration. Answer the questions **in English**.

(a) What had Cecilia arranged to do? .... *(1 mark)*

(b) What was the surprise? Give **two** details. ....

.... *(2 marks)*

(c) What did she enjoy the most? .... *(1 mark)*

(d) How do we know she will remember the day? .... *(1 mark)*

Directions

26 Directions

Read Alejandro's note.

> Me has preguntado dónde está la panadería y cuál es el camino más corto. ¡Pues es muy sencillo! Sigue estas instrucciones:
>
> 1) Vete hasta el semáforo.
>
> 2) Cruza la calle.
>
> 3) Coge la primera calle a la izquierda.

Part A

What has Alejandro been asked? Write the correct two letters in the boxes.

A	Where is the bakery.
B	Where is the bridge.

C	How to get there.
D	How long it takes to get there.

☐ ☐

(2 marks)

Part B

Write the correct **three** letters of the pictures that match Alejandro's instructions in each box.

| A | B | C | D | E | F |

☐ ☐ ☐

(3 marks)

27 Finding the way

What do these people have to do?

A	B	C
Turn left.	Go straight ahead.	Go up the road.

D	E	F
Take the first right.	Cross the square.	Cross the bridge.

Listen and write the correct letter in each box.

1	Pepe	☐	*(1 mark)*	3	Lázaro	☐	*(1 mark)*
2	Juani	☐	*(1 mark)*	4	Jimena	☐	*(1 mark)*

Transport

28 Cycling safely

Read what this advert says.

¡Ya sabes las ventajas de tener una bici – es el modo de transporte más limpio, más barato y más ecológico que puedes usar!

Pero …

¿Has llevado tu bici al taller?

¿Cuándo fue la última vez que la llevaste a revisión?

¿Sabes que miles de accidentes cada año se deben al uso de bicicletas en mal estado?

No seas una cifra más – llévala ya – ¡más vale prevenir!

Part A

Choose the phrase which best describes what the advert is doing. Write the correct letter in the box.

A	Encouraging people to be more environmentally friendly by travelling on a bike.
B	Persuading people to buy a new bike.
C	Emphasising the importance of keeping your bike in good repair.

☐   *(1 mark)*

Part B

What **three** advantages of having a bicycle does the advertisement mention? Answer **in English**.

1 ....   *(1 mark)*

2 ....   *(1 mark)*

3 ....   *(1 mark)*

29 Means of transport

Which mode of transport does each advertisement promote?

A	motorcycle	C	boat	E	on foot	G	train
B	underground	D	car	F	bus	H	plane

Listen and write the correct letter in each box.

1 ☐ *(1 mark)*   2 ☐ *(1 mark)*   3 ☐ *(1 mark)*   4 ☐ *(1 mark)*

> Think of the transport words **before** you listen, then you will be better prepared.

At the train station

30 Travelling in Spain

Read Chico's email about travelling in Spain. Then answer the questions **in English**.

○○○   ⊂⊃

🚫   ↩   ↩   ↪   🖨
Borrar   Responder   Responder   Adelante   Imprimir
                      a todas

¡Hola, Sole!

Estoy deseando que vengas a visitar a mi familia. Todos quieren conocerte. No te preocupes por el viaje – es muy fácil.

Sólo tienes que irte a la estación de trenes unos días antes del viaje. Vete tranquilamente a la máquina y pulsa la tecla que pone 'billetes de ida y vuelta'. Te pedirá tu destino, y entonces pulsa hasta que te dé la opción de Santiago de Compostela. ¡Estate segura de elegir el destino adecuado! Te dará la opción de primera o segunda clase. Selecciona segunda – es más barato. Introduce el dinero – puedes pagar con dinero o con tarjeta. Recoge tus dos billetes, el recibo y el cambio – ¡y ya está!

Te estaré esperando en el andén.

Chico ☺

(a) What is the purpose of Chico's email? .... *(1 mark)*

(b) What type of ticket should Sole buy? .... *(1 mark)*

(c) Why does Sole have to be careful? .... *(1 mark)*

(d) Why does Chico recommend choosing second class? .... *(1 mark)*

(e) What payment options are available? Mention **two** things. ....

.... *(2 marks)*

(f) What is Chico going to do? .... *(1 mark)*

31 At the train station

Catarina is at the train station.

For question (c), work out the **Spanish** for the numbers before you listen.

Listen and complete these statements. Write the correct letter in each box.

(a) She wants to buy …

A	a ticket to Valencia.
B	two tickets to Valencia.
C	a ticket to Barcelona.

☐ *(1 mark)*

(b) She doesn't want …

A	first class.
B	a reserved seat.
C	a one-way ticket.

☐ *(1 mark)*

(c) She has to pay …

A	35 euros.
B	25 euros.
C	13 euros.

☐ *(1 mark)*

(d) They might be held up by …

A	the weather.
B	work on the line.
C	cancellations.

☐ *(1 mark)*

Had a go ☐   Nearly there ☐   Nailed it! ☐

News headlines

32 Destructive fires

Read this newspaper article.

Varios incendios de verano desafortunados en España han dejado un muerto y tres heridos en Alicante.

La víctima mortal es un joven estudiante de 17 años – considerado ahora un héroe debido a su valor – que falleció participando en la extinción del incendio declarado en Torremanzanas.

En las islas Canarias, los fuegos en Tenerife y La Gomera han obligado a evacuar a más de 4000 vecinos. Se cree que la mayor parte de los fuegos han sido causados por personas que tiran las colillas de los cigarrillos por las ventanillas de sus coches.

Más de la mitad de los incendios de este año han dañado zonas forestales protegidas.

According to the article, which statement is true? Write the correct letter in each box.

(a)

A	A member of the public died trying to put out a fire.
B	A member of the public was wounded trying to put out a fire.
C	Three people have died in the fires.

☐ *(1 mark)*

(c)

A	The causes of the fires are as yet unknown.
B	Careless people are believed to have caused the fires.
C	It is thought the fires have been started deliberately.

☐ *(1 mark)*

(b)

A	Thousands of homes have been damaged.
B	Thousands of vehicles have been destroyed.
C	Thousands of people have had to leave their homes.

☐ *(1 mark)*

(d)

A	Villages have been destroyed.
B	Mainly conservation areas have been affected.
C	Mainly residential areas have been affected.

☐ *(1 mark)*

33 The lost generation

Listen to this news report.

Have the following gone up, gone down or remained the same?

(a) youth employment in Spain .... *(1 mark)*

(b) standard of education of young people .... *(1 mark)*

(c) their ambitions and plans .... *(1 mark)*

(d) their hope .... *(1 mark)*

(e) youth emigration .... *(1 mark)*

The environment

34 What worries you the most?

Read what these young people say about the environment.

Lo que más me preocupa es la cantidad de población que hay en el mundo. Debemos hacer algo. No tenemos recursos suficientes para sostenerlos y es cada vez más difícil alimentarlos. Si seguimos así, nos quedaremos sin nada, lo cual sería una catástrofe.

Amara

El problema global más grave para mí es la manera en la que estamos destruyendo el planeta. Si no paramos de dañar la capa de ozono debido a la contaminación, habrá una tragedia. Hay que parar de hacerlo.

Bernardo

Read these statements. Write whether **A** (Amara), **B** (Bernardo), or **A/B** (both Amara and Bernardo) refer to each topic.

(a) If something isn't done there will be serious consequences. ☐ *(1 mark)*

(b) The biggest problem is that there aren't enough resources to go around. ☐ *(1 mark)*

(c) The main problem is related to climate. ☐ *(1 mark)*

(d) The main problem is related to farming. ☐ *(1 mark)*

(e) We need to act. ☐ *(1 mark)*

35 Global issues

Which opinion is each person expressing? Listen and write the correct letters in the boxes.

(a) War …

A	can never be stopped so why try?
B	is part of life's rich tapestry.
C	could be ended by working together.

☐ *(1 mark)*

(b) Poverty …

A	has no solution.
B	is the fault of the poor.
C	needs the help of the rich.

☐ *(1 mark)*

(c) Deforestation …

A	is dying out.
B	has a knock-on effect.
C	helps animals.

☐ *(1 mark)*

(d) Global warming …

A	is caused by acid rain.
B	is affected by the weather.
C	is responsible for freak weather.

☐ *(1 mark)*

Environmental issues

36 Borja's research

Read what Borja says about what his community is doing to help the environment.

Para mis deberes he tenido que investigar lo que hacemos en nuestro barrio para contribuir a la protección del medio ambiente.

En el pueblo donde vivo llevamos mucho tiempo reciclando la basura, pero aunque han puesto contenedores diferentes el ayuntamiento dice que ha bajado la cantidad de residuos que reciclamos.

Muchas de las pequeñas tiendas de mi zona han empezado a reducir las cuentas unos céntimos para los clientes que traen sus propias bolsas de plástico, así que hemos reducido nuestro consumo de esa materia.

Me sorprendió también que hay menos amigos míos que compran ropa y cosas de segunda mano. Ahora son menos, mientras que hace poco era algo bastante popular.

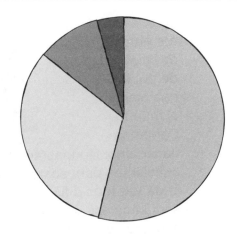

Desafortunadamente, lo que sigue igual es nuestro consumo de electricidad. He hablado con mucha gente y todos dicen lo mismo. Como no tienen dinero para salir, se quedan en casa y ven la tele. ¡Eso gasta energía, claro, y nuestro consumo ha aumentado un poco!

Borja

For each activity, write whether it has gone up, gone down or remained the same.

1 recycling .... *(1 mark)*

2 use of plastic bags .... *(1 mark)*

3 buying second-hand clothes .... *(1 mark)*

4 electricity consumption .... *(1 mark)*

37 News report

Listen to this news report about throwing away gadgets. Complete the sentences by writing the correct letter in each box.

(a) We throw away gadgets because …

A	we want the latest things.
B	things aren't made to last.
C	we need more than one item.

☐ *(1 mark)*

(b) These gadgets …

A	end up in landfill.
B	aren't cheap to replace.
C	can't be reused.

☐ *(1 mark)*

(c) It is a problem because the gadgets are …

A	dangerous.
B	expensive.
C	not out of date.

☐ *(1 mark)*

(d) The solution is to …

A	mend them.
B	send them abroad.
C	crush them.

☐ *(1 mark)*

What I do to be 'green'

38 Eva's environmental club

Read this article Eva has written for her school magazine.

Murcia

Estoy orgullosa de ser miembro del club de ecologistas del cole. Nos reunimos cada martes después de clase y nos dedicamos a hacer artículos de joyería y otros objetos con basura que reciclamos.

Somos muy creativos y compartimos el deseo de reducir el desperdicio de materias que son, en realidad, reciclables.

Carlos, por ejemplo, construye tablas de monopatín con maderas que han tirado y otras cosas que encuentra en los contenedores del pueblo. Las decora y hasta ha empezado a venderlas. Yo, por mi parte, hago anillos y collares con el cristal de botellas desechadas.

Creemos que, en vez de quejarnos, todos deberíamos hacer algo positivo por el medio ambiente.

Eva Sánchez

Complete these statements. Write the correct letter in each box.

(a) Eva and her friends …

A	make things.
B	clear away rubbish.
C	buy recycled things.

☐ *(1 mark)*

(b) They share a desire to …

A	save money.
B	protest about waste.
C	recycle unwanted items.

☐ *(1 mark)*

(c) Carlos makes things out of material he …

A	produces.
B	finds.
C	has broken.

☐ *(1 mark)*

(d) They believe people should stop …

A	buying new things.
B	using materials that can't be recycled.
C	complaining.

☐ *(1 mark)*

39 'Green' schools

Listen to Gloria and Ricardo talk about their schools. Who mentions the following?

Write **G** (Gloria), **R** (Ricardo) or **G/R** (both Gloria and Ricardo) in each box.

(a) My school is concerned with saving energy. ☐ *(1 mark)*

(b) My school keeps track of how much energy we produce. ☐ *(1 mark)*

(c) My school recycles. ☐ *(1 mark)*

(d) My school's efforts are unique in our area. ☐ *(1 mark)*

(e) My school grows several different things. ☐ *(1 mark)*

(f) My school sometimes stops using energy completely. ☐ *(1 mark)*

School subjects

1 Which subject?

Which subject is being discussed?

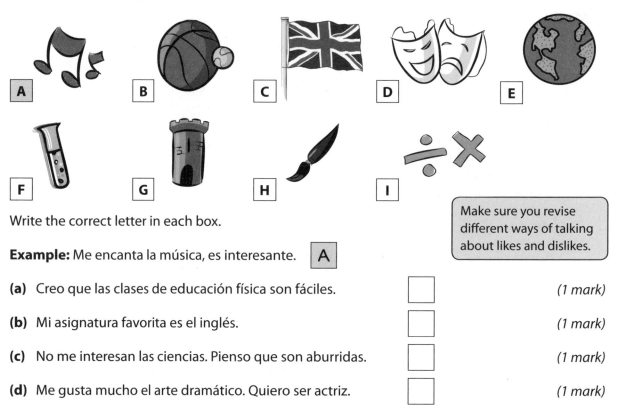

Write the correct letter in each box.

Example: Me encanta la música, es interesante.   A

> Make sure you revise different ways of talking about likes and dislikes.

(a) Creo que las clases de educación física son fáciles.   ☐   *(1 mark)*

(b) Mi asignatura favorita es el inglés.   ☐   *(1 mark)*

(c) No me interesan las ciencias. Pienso que son aburridas.   ☐   *(1 mark)*

(d) Me gusta mucho el arte dramático. Quiero ser actriz.   ☐   *(1 mark)*

2 Ana's subject preferences

Listen to Ana talking about her lessons at school. Which **four** of the statements are true?

A	Ana studies hard at school.
B	She doesn't mind studying ICT.
C	She prefers ICT to art.
D	She doesn't like maths.
E	She has fewer periods of drama than art each week.
F	She finds chemistry interesting.
G	She likes her science teacher.
H	She enjoys PE.
I	She is only physically active at the weekends.
J	Her favourite subjects are languages.

Write the correct letters in the boxes.

☐ ☐ ☐ ☐

(4 marks)

School description

C

READING

3 Paco's new school

Read Paco's thoughts on his new school. What topic is he referring to each time?

A	Cada clase dura cincuenta minutos.
B	Durante el recreo jugamos en el patio.
C	Tenemos que llegar por la mañana a las ocho.
D	¡Hay tanta gente en el patio durante el recreo!
E	Los profesores siempre respetan a los alumnos.
F	Tenemos que seguir reglas distintas en cada clase.
G	El recreo dura un cuarto de hora.
H	Los alumnos respetan a todos los profesores.
I	Las clases terminan a las cuatro.
J	Siempre voy al colegio a pie.
K	Cada clase empieza con actividades orales.

Write the correct letter in each box.

Example: arrival time C

(a) teachers' attitude towards pupils ☐ *(1 mark)*

(b) length of each lesson ☐ *(1 mark)*

(c) what pupils do during breaks ☐ *(1 mark)*

(d) class rules ☐ *(1 mark)*

(e) class routines ☐ *(1 mark)*

C

LISTENING

59

4 Daniel talks about his school

Listen to Daniel talking about his school. What does he think of the following aspects?

Write **P** (positive), **N** (negative) or **P + N** (both positive and negative) in each space in the grid.

Example: the buildings	P + N
(a) the classrooms	
(b) the playground	
(c) the laboratories	
(d) the students	
(e) the sports facilities	
(f) the changing rooms	

(1 mark) (for a–f each)

School routine

5 A typical school day

Read what people say about their school routine.

> **Susana:** Empezamos a las ocho de la mañana. Tenemos siete horas de clase al día. En mi opinión, es un buen colegio, pero los profesores nos ponen demasiados deberes, así que no tengo mucho tiempo libre. Me encanta trabajar con los ordenadores. Tengo la informática dos veces a la semana. ¡Es genial! Prefiero los jueves porque no hay clase de ciencias.
>
> **Tere:** Siempre me levanto temprano porque tengo que ir al colegio en autobús y no me gusta llegar con retraso. Soy trabajadora y mis mejores asignaturas son las ciencias y los idiomas. También tenemos muchas actividades después del cole. Hay dos clases antes y dos después del recreo, que dura un cuarto de hora. A mediodía siempre voy a casa de un amigo para comer.
>
> **Arantxa:** No me gusta mucho mi colegio y creo que hay demasiadas reglas que hay que respetar. Hay mucha variedad con respecto a lo que se puede estudiar, pero en general las clases son poco interesantes. Mi padre es profesor en el mismo colegio. Está muy bien porque por la mañana vamos juntos al colegio en su coche. Lo malo es que aunque el día no es largo y terminamos a las tres, tengo que esperar a mi padre antes de poder volver a casa.

Read the statements. Who is speaking? Write **S** (Susana), **T** (Tere) or **A** (Arantxa) in each box.

Example: I have seven hours of school a day. ☐ S

(a) I go to school by car.   ☐   *(1 mark)*

(b) I'm good at languages.   ☐   *(1 mark)*

(c) I find the lessons boring.   ☐   *(1 mark)*

(d) My school day is too long.   ☐   *(1 mark)*

(e) I don't enjoy science.   ☐   *(1 mark)*

(f) I enjoy extracurricular activities.   ☐   *(1 mark)*

6 A school day

Listen to Andrés describing a typical school day. Answer the questions in English.

Example: What time does school normally start? ....8:15...

(a) What day does Andrés refer to? .... *(1 mark)*

(b) Why was he late for school? .... *(1 mark)*

(c) What did he do at break time? .... *(1 mark)*

(d) Where did Andrés have lunch? .... *(1 mark)*

Comparing schools

7 My school exchange

Read this blog about Rafaela's recent school exchange trip.

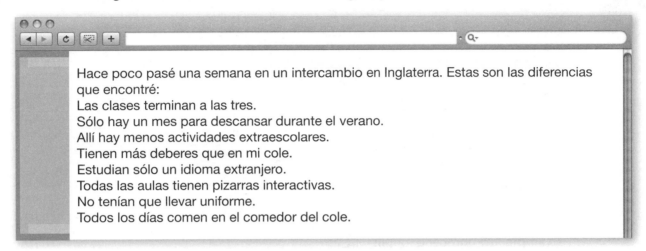

Hace poco pasé una semana en un intercambio en Inglaterra. Estas son las diferencias que encontré:
Las clases terminan a las tres.
Sólo hay un mes para descansar durante el verano.
Allí hay menos actividades extraescolares.
Tienen más deberes que en mi cole.
Estudian sólo un idioma extranjero.
Todas las aulas tienen pizarras interactivas.
No tenían que llevar uniforme.
Todos los días comen en el comedor del cole.

Which **four** of the statements below are mentioned in the text? Write the correct letters in the boxes.

A	Rafaela spent a month at the school.	E	They have good ICT equipment.
B	Summer holidays are shorter.	F	They don't have to do homework.
C	Extracurricular activities are limited.	G	They can wear whatever they like.
D	They study more than one language.	H	They have lunch at school.

☐ ☐ ☐ ☐

(4 marks)

8 English schools

Listen to Conchi talk about English schools. Which **four** statements below summarise her opinions?

A	The school day is too long.
B	There's too much homework.
C	Spanish is well taught.
D	School uniforms are a good idea.
E	The catering facilities are excellent.
F	The facilities are good.
G	Lots of pupils stay behind after lessons in the English school.
H	The school day is shorter in England.
I	The break times are too short.

Write the **four** correct letters in the boxes.

☐ ☐ ☐ ☐

(4 marks)

At primary school

9 Opinions on primary schools

Read these opinions on primary schools.

A	Tenía muchos amigos.
B	Siempre había buena ayuda en clase.
C	Había menos alumnos.
D	Siempre estudiaba inglés y matemáticas.
E	Estudiaba menos asignaturas.
F	Iba andando a la escuela.
G	Las clases duraban cuarenta minutos.

H	Me encantaba jugar con las mascotas.
I	Cada verano íbamos de excursión.
J	No tenía que llevar uniforme.
K	Todos respetábamos las reglas.

> If you don't recognise some of these irregular verbs, concentrate on the rest of the sentence as this is where the answer can be found.

Which sentence above does each of the following refer to? Write the correct letter in each box.

Example: the number of pupils C

(a) teacher support ☐ *(1 mark)*   **(d)** general behaviour ☐ *(1 mark)*

(b) length of each lesson ☐ *(1 mark)*   **(e)** daily classwork ☐ *(1 mark)*

(c) breadth of study ☐ *(1 mark)*

10 Primary school memories

Listen to these young people talking about their primary schools. Complete the sentences by writing the correct letter in each box.

Example: At break Begoña …

A	drank fruit juice.
B	ate some fruit.
C	bought a sandwich.

B

(a) Pablo says being in the primary school football team was …

A	compulsory.
B	just like his school now.
C	a choice.

☐ *(1 mark)*

(b) Juanita found primary school …

A	fun.
B	easy.
C	interesting.

☐ *(1 mark)*

(c) Cesc enjoyed …

A	art.
B	literacy.
C	numeracy.

☐ *(1 mark)*

(d) Gerardo says the classes were …

A	very big.
B	not big enough.
C	very small.

☐ *(1 mark)*

Rules at school

11 Martín's schoool rules

Read this letter from Martín. What school rules does he refer to and why?

¡Hola!

En mi colegio las cosas han cambiado. Ahora tenemos que llevar uniforme y dicen que el año que viene van a prohibir llevar maquillaje y joyas. Tampoco se puede comer chicle, pero la comida del comedor es horrible y siempre me como un chicle después de comer. Los profesores no son muy estrictos, pero sólo nos dejan usar móviles en el patio. Los ordenadores son mejores y nos dejan mandar correos electrónicos.

Todavía hay problemas con algunos alumnos que son maleducados y no estudian todo lo que es debido, pero su comportamiento es mejor y en el cole hay un ambiente agradable.

Saludos, Martín

Complete the grids by writing a rule or a reason for it **in English**.

(a)

Rule	Reason
uniform this year	

(1 mark)

(b)

Rule	Reason
uniform next year	

(1 mark)

(c)

Rule	Reason
	eating restrictions

(1 mark)

(d)

Rule	Reason
mobile phones	

(1 mark)

(e)

Rule	Reason
computers	

(1 mark)

(f)

Rule	Reason
	improvements made

(1 mark)

12 María talks about her school

Listen to María talking about the rules in her school. Answer the questions **in English**.

Part 1

(a) What do the students have to do before class starts? .... *(1 mark)*

(b) What happened to María when she didn't do this? .... *(1 mark)*

(c) In which circumstances does María agree with the rule about earrings?

.... *(1 mark)*

Part 2

(d) What does María think is dangerous? .... *(1 mark)*

(e) Which rule does she think is ridiculous? Why? .... *(2 marks)*

(f) Which rule does she talk about last and what does she think of this rule?

.... *(2 marks)*

71

Problems at school

13 Problems at school

Read what some young people say about problems at school. What are they writing about?

A	examination timetables
B	homework
C	getting too many detentions
D	not having friends
E	being bullied at school
F	people being rude
G	pressure to do well
H	losing friends
I	concentrating in lessons
J	fighting at school

> Answer the questions you are sure about first and cross out the options as you use them. Then come back to the others.

Write the correct letter in each box.

(a) Algunos alumnos intimidan a otros y a veces tengo miedo.
☐ *(1 mark)*

(b) Lo que me preocupa en el colegio es que soy tímido y no tengo amigos.
☐ *(1 mark)*

(c) Es difícil trabajar porque me molestan los otros alumnos.
☐ *(1 mark)*

(d) Mis padres esperan mucho de mí, pero creo que voy a fracasar.
☐ *(1 mark)*

(e) No puedo repasar los apuntes porque es imposible trabajar en casa.
☐ *(1 mark)*

14 School life

Listen to these young people talking about school life. What problems do they identify? Make notes in the grid **in English**.

Example: Carolina	Some boys intimidate other students.	
(a) Juan		*(1 mark)*
(b) Sergio		*(1 mark)*
(c) Cristina		*(1 mark)*
(d) Iker		*(1 mark)*
(e) Ana		*(1 mark)*

Future education plans

15 Opinions about education

Read these descriptions of people's future plans.

Maxi:

> Voy a seguir estudiando en mi instituto y después espero ir a la universidad. La educación es muy importante para mí. Me encantan los idiomas y quiero estudiarlos. Espero sacar buenas notas. Dos años más en el cole ¡no es demasiado!

Carla:

> Creo que nos preocupamos demasiado por el futuro. Siempre hay tiempo para estudiar. No estoy segura, pero me gustaría tomar un año sabático antes de hacer mis exámenes.

Alberto:

> No quiero seguir estudiando en el colegio. Es aburrido. Intento encontrar un trabajo. Lo ideal para mí sería trabajar y estudiar a la vez.

Read the statements and decide who says each one. Write **M** (Maxi), **C** (Carla) or **A** (Alberto) in each box.

Example: I want to go to university.   M

(a) I'd like to find a job.   ☐   *(1 mark)*

(b) I'd like a year off school.   ☐   *(1 mark)*

(c) I think languages are important.   ☐   *(1 mark)*

(d) I don't enjoy school.   ☐   *(1 mark)*

(e) I'm undecided.   ☐   *(1 mark)*

(f) I'm going to stay at school.   ☐   *(1 mark)*

16 Future subjects

Listen to these young people talking about their plans. What school subjects do they need to focus on? Write the correct answer **in English** on each line.

Example: Mario ..... *cookery* ....

(a) Raquel .... *(1 mark)*

(b) Enrique .... *(1 mark)*

(c) Sabrina .... *(1 mark)*

(d) Rafa .... *(1 mark)*

(e) Ángel .... *(1 mark)*

Future plans

17 Patricia's plans

Read Patricia's letter about her future plans. Answer the questions below **in English**.

> ¡Hola Miguel!
>
> Acabo de terminar mis exámenes y estoy completamente exhausta. No tenía ni idea de lo difícil que es repasar tantas cosas. Si saco buenas notas, voy a seguir estudiando. Espero ir a la universidad para hacer una carrera de idiomas – alemán o quizás inglés – todavía no estoy segura.
>
> Lo bueno de vivir en la ciudad es que podré quedarme en casa con mis padres. Nos llevamos muy bien y me ayudarán con el coste de la vida universitaria. Podré estudiar y ahorrar a la vez, ¡qué guay!
>
> En cuanto termine la universidad, me gustaría buscar un trabajo en Londres porque dicen que la vida nocturna es genial y necesitaré un poco de diversión.
>
> ¡Chao por ahora! Patricia

(a) What surprised Patricia most about studying for her examinations?

.... *(1 mark)*

(b) How does she feel about her future plans? Write the correct letter in the box.

A	worried	**B**	unclear	**C**	unhappy

☐ *(1 mark)*

(c) What does Patricia say about living at home? Give a reason for your answer.

.... *(2 marks)*

(d) What does Patricia say about working in London? Give a reason for your answer.

.... *(2 marks)*

18 Future careers

Listen to some young people talking about their future careers. Write the correct letter in each box.

(a) What aspect of work is important to Borja?

A	His hours
B	His salary
C	His colleagues

☐ *(1 mark)*

(c) What does Jesús refer to?

A	Career and success
B	Love and marriage
C	Fame and fortune

☐ *(1 mark)*

(b) What aspect of work would María enjoy most?

A	The company
B	The social benefits
C	The tasks

☐ *(1 mark)*

(d) In what sector would Ana like to work?

A	Nursing
B	Child care
C	Education

☐ *(1 mark)*

Jobs

19 Different jobs

Look at these pictures of jobs.

Which jobs are described below? Write the correct letter in each box.

Example: Soy enfermera.　F

(a) Mi padre trabaja como cocinero.　☐　*(1 mark)*

(b) Mi hermana mayor es secretaria.　☐　*(1 mark)*

(c) Mi padre es cartero.　☐　*(1 mark)*

(d) Los sábados trabajo como peluquero.　☐　*(1 mark)*

20 My father's job

Inés is talking about her father's job. Complete the sentences by putting the correct letter in each box.

Example: Inés's father works in a …

A	hospital.
B	kitchen.
C	bank.

A

> Make sure you listen right to the end of the passage before you answer the questions. Listen out carefully for words such as *pero* (but).

(a) He finds his work …

A	tiring.
B	dull.
C	difficult.

☐ *(1 mark)*

(b) He travels to work …

A	by bus.
B	by car.
C	on foot.

☐ *(1 mark)*

(c) He prefers working with …

A	babies.
B	children.
C	older people.

☐ *(1 mark)*

(d) He finds the salary …

A	good enough.
B	not enough.
C	really good.

☐ *(1 mark)*

Job adverts

21 Employment offers

Read the following job adverts.

> Empleo administrativo en una empresa del centro ciudad. Buen sueldo. De lunes a viernes, **9 – 17 horas.**

> Se necesita limpiador de piscinas a tiempo parcial en el polideportivo municipal. Fines de semana de 10 a 18 horas. **Sueldo 12 euros la hora.**

> Trabajo jornada completa en un restaurante. Toda la semana menos los domingos. Paga 20 euros la hora. Entrevistas la semana que viene.

> Se busca dependiente con experiencia para tienda de ropa. Horario: martes a viernes de 9 a 6. Descuento de 10% en compras.

Which **four** statements are true? Write the correct letters in the boxes.

(a) The sports centre is looking for someone to clean the pool.

(b) None of the jobs is full-time.

(c) A shop is looking for a sales assistant.

(d) There is a discount for workers at the restaurant.

(e) The office work pays 15 euros per hour.

(f) The office is in the town centre.

(g) The restaurant is not open on Sundays.

(h) The job in the shop is for 5 days a week.

☐ ☐ ☐ ☐

(4 marks)

> Don't lose marks by giving too much information. Look carefully at the number of points you need to provide.

22 A radio advert

Listen to the radio advert. Answer the questions **in English**.

(a) When would the work start? .... *(1 mark)*

(b) What type of work is on offer? .... *(1 mark)*

(c) What is the prospective employer looking for in applicants? Name **two** things.

....

.... *(2 marks)*

(d) What might make the job attractive to listeners? Name **two** things.

....

.... *(2 marks)*

(e) What would be the next step for prospective candidates?

.... *(1 mark)*

CV

23 Paz's application letter

Read Paz's letter of application for a job.

- Tengo veintiséis años y nací el dos de febrero de mil novecientos noventa y ocho.

- He trabajado durante cinco años como traductora para varias editoriales internacionales. De momento tengo un contrato con Casa Alianza. Durante mis estudios en una universidad estadounidense tuve varios empleos diferentes.

- He hecho varios cursos de informática. Tengo carné de conducir y varias medallas de deporte.

- Adjunto una carta del director de mi instituto y una del jefe de mi empresa actual. Podría conseguir más referencias en caso necesario.

- Soy una persona entusiasta, muy educada y con buena presencia. Con la gente me llevo bien, aunque prefiero trabajar sola. Tanto mis profesores del colegio, como mis jefes hablan bien de mí y de mis esfuerzos en clase o en el trabajo. Me interesa viajar.

Answer the questions in **English**.

(a) What information does Paz include to show she is good at languages? .... *(1 mark)*

(b) Where has she worked abroad? .... *(1 mark)*

(c) Which of Paz's achievements suggest she would be good at a very active job?

.... *(1 mark)*

(d) Who does Paz provide references from? Mention **two** things.

.... *(2 marks)*

(e) Why wouldn't a job leading an international team be suitable for Paz?

.... *(1 mark)*

24 A job interview

Listen to this interview with señor Alonso. Answer the questions **in English**.

(a) Why, according to señor Alonso, is it important to have a good CV?

.... *(1 mark)*

(b) What does he say you should include? Name **two** things.

.... *(2 marks)*

(c) What does he say you should be careful with? Name **two** things.

.... *(2 marks)*

(d) What does he say about a one-fits-all CV? .... *(1 mark)*

(e) What does he say you should do before starting to write your CV?

.... *(1 mark)*

(f) How can this affect your CV? .... *(1 mark)*

Had a go ☐   Nearly there ☐   Nailed it! ☐

Job application

25 Rosa applies for a job

Read Rosa's letter of application. Answer the questions below **in English**.

> Muy señor mío:
>
> He visto su anuncio en el periódico del barrio y le escribo para solicitar el puesto de dependienta en su tienda de ropa.
>
> Tengo mucho interés en un puesto como éste porque me gustaría entrar en el sector del comercio. Hace poco acabé los estudios de secundaria y ahora busco un trabajo de verano antes de ir a la universidad en otoño. Hice mis prácticas laborales en una agencia de viajes y he tenido varios empleos en hoteles del vecindario.
>
> Como se puede ver en el currículum que le mando adjunto, destaco en las asignaturas de informática y comercio y además, domino el francés y el inglés. Soy trabajadora, honesta y puntual. Estoy disponible para empezar inmediatamente.
>
> Esperando su respuesta para concertar una entrevista,
>
> Le saluda atentamente,
>
> Rosa Martínez

(a) Where did Rosa find out about this job? .... *(1 mark)*

(b) Where would she be working? .... *(1 mark)*

(c) When does she want to work and why? ....
.... *(2 marks)*

(d) Give **two** details about her previous work experiences.
.... *(2 marks)*

(e) What does she say about languages? .... *(1 mark)*

(f) Mention **one** thing she says about her personal qualities.
.... *(1 mark)*

26 Paco's personal details

Paco is being interviewed for a job. Listen and complete the details in the grid **in English**.

Example: surname	López	
(a) age		*(1 mark)*
(b) job applied for		*(1 mark)*
(c) best school subjects		*(1 mark)*
(d) personal qualities		*(1 mark)*

Job interview

27 Carolina's job interview

Read this email from Carolina about a job interview. Answer the questions below **in English**.

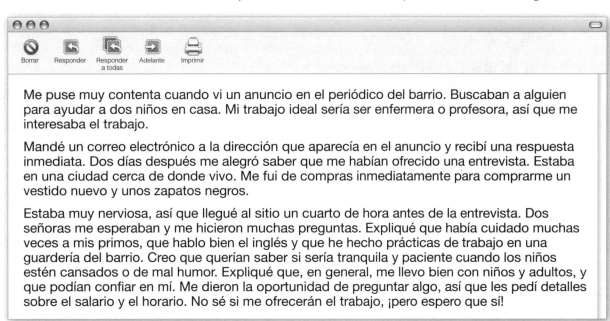

Me puse muy contenta cuando vi un anuncio en el periódico del barrio. Buscaban a alguien para ayudar a dos niños en casa. Mi trabajo ideal sería ser enfermera o profesora, así que me interesaba el trabajo.

Mandé un correo electrónico a la dirección que aparecía en el anuncio y recibí una respuesta inmediata. Dos días después me alegró saber que me habían ofrecido una entrevista. Estaba en una ciudad cerca de donde vivo. Me fui de compras inmediatamente para comprarme un vestido nuevo y unos zapatos negros.

Estaba muy nerviosa, así que llegué al sitio un cuarto de hora antes de la entrevista. Dos señoras me esperaban y me hicieron muchas preguntas. Expliqué que había cuidado muchas veces a mis primos, que hablo bien el inglés y que he hecho prácticas de trabajo en una guardería del barrio. Creo que querían saber si sería tranquila y paciente cuando los niños estén cansados o de mal humor. Expliqué que, en general, me llevo bien con niños y adultos, y que podían confiar en mí. Me dieron la oportunidad de preguntar algo, así que les pedí detalles sobre el salario y el horario. No sé si me ofrecerán el trabajo, ¡pero espero que sí!

(a) What did the advertised job involve?

.... *(1 mark)*

(b) How would the job help her future work plans?

.... *(1 mark)*

(c) What did she do that shows she wasn't completely confident about the interview?

.... *(1 mark)*

(d) What did she say to convince the interviewers of her ability to cope in difficult situations?

Mention **two** details. ....

.... *(2 marks)*

(e) What was her attitude to the job after the interview? .... *(1 mark)*

28 José's interview

Listen to José being interviewed for a job. Answer the questions **in English**.

Part 1

(a) Where does José want to work? .... *(1 mark)*

(b) What experience has he had? .... *(1 mark)*

(c) Where did he see the job advertised? .... *(1 mark)*

Part 2

(d) What does he say are his best qualities? Give **two** details. ....

.... *(2 marks)*

(e) When could he start the job? .... *(1 mark)*

(f) When will he be told if he's got it? .... *(1 mark)*

Opinions about jobs

29 Ronaldo's working life

Read what Ronaldo has to say about his working life.

> Me llamo Ronaldo y nací en Argentina, pero llevo cinco años trabajando en el barrio de Leganés, en Madrid. Mi esposa es madrileña. Para mí es mucho mejor trabajar aquí porque el transporte público es excelente y puedo ir en metro. Lo malo es que vivo bastante lejos así que tengo que levantarme a las seis de la mañana. Soy enfermero y trabajo con niños. Lo que más aprecio de mi trabajo es el contacto con la gente y trabajar en equipo. Sin embargo, suelo trabajar muchas horas y las tareas me parecen difíciles. La mayoría de los pacientes son amables y mis compañeros de trabajo también. A la hora de comer nos gusta ir a alguno de los bares de tapas de la zona. Madrid es famosa por sus buenos restaurantes.

Answer the questions. Write the correct letter in each box.

(a) Ronaldo has been in this job …

A	since he began his career in Argentina.
B	for a number of years.
C	since he got married.

☐ *(1 mark)*

(b) He refers to the transport system as …

A	slow.
B	expensive.
C	efficient.

☐ *(1 mark)*

(c) Ronaldo appreciates …

A	the working hours.
B	the team work.
C	looking after members of his family.

☐ *(1 mark)*

(d) Lunch times are usually spent with …

A	patients.
B	colleagues.
C	friends.

☐ *(1 mark)*

30 Job likes and dislikes

Listen to these young people talking about jobs. Identity the job and give the reason why they like it.

	Jobs		Reasons
A	nurse	G	interesting
B	electrician	H	flexible working hours
C	gardener	I	varied
D	writer	J	stimulating
E	waiter	K	in the open air
F	engineer	L	easy

Write the correct letters in the grid.

	Job	Reason	
1			*(2 marks)*
2			*(2 marks)*
3			*(2 marks)*

Part-time jobs

31 A holiday job

Read Freya's account of a holiday job.

> Vivo en Puerto de la Cruz, que se encuentra a orillas del mar. Nunca había pensado que mi trabajo de verano sería tan agradable. Me encontraba muy bien cada mañana yendo al trabajo. Tenía que cuidar las bicicletas y yo era la única persona en la oficina. ¡Qué suerte!
>
> La gente de vacaciones tenía la costumbre de alquilar las bicis bastante temprano por la mañana y no las delvolvían hasta las seis o así – justo cuando cerraba la oficina. Durante el día no tenía casi nada de trabajo excepto en ocasiones escasas cuando había que reparar algo. Así que para pasar el tiempo tomaba el sol en la playa, que estaba a menos de veinte metros. Me gustaba mucho charlar con los clientes y aconsejarles sobre los sitios de interés que podrían visitar.
>
> Por las tardes algo que me molestaba era tener que lavar las bicis antes de cerrar la tienda. La única otra cosa inconveniente que encontraba difícil de superar era que había que tratar amablemente a los niños – incluso a los maleducados. Menos mal que tres cuartos de los niños eran simpáticos. Sin embargo, creo que no me gustaría ser profesora …

Answer the questions **in English**.

(a) What surprised Freya about her holiday job?

.... *(1 mark)*

(b) Who did she work with?

.... *(1 mark)*

(c) How hard did she find the job and why?

.... *(2 marks)*

(d) As well as looking after the bikes, what additional service did she provide?

.... *(1 mark)*

(e) What is her attitude to children? Give **two** details.

.... *(2 marks)*

32 Part-time jobs

Listen to these young people talking about their part-time jobs. What does each person do?

Write the correct letter in each box.

A	B	C	D
sorting out clothes	working in a restaurant	washing cars	doing housework

E	F	G	H
delivering newspapers	working in a sports centre	working on a farm	babysitting

Example: H

1 ☐ *(1 mark)*   **2** ☐ *(1 mark)*   **3** ☐ *(1 mark)*   **4** ☐ *(1 mark)*

My work experience

33 Juan's work experience

Read this email from Juan about his work experience.

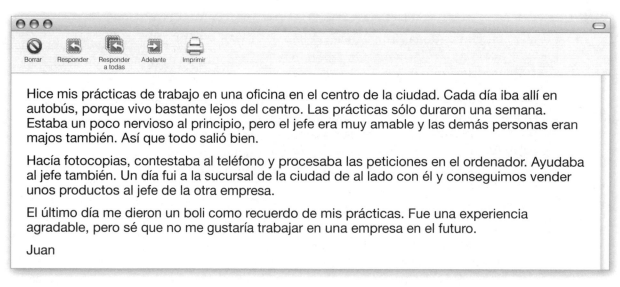

Hice mis prácticas de trabajo en una oficina en el centro de la ciudad. Cada día iba allí en autobús, porque vivo bastante lejos del centro. Las prácticas sólo duraron una semana. Estaba un poco nervioso al principio, pero el jefe era muy amable y las demás personas eran majos también. Así que todo salió bien.

Hacía fotocopias, contestaba al teléfono y procesaba las peticiones en el ordenador. Ayudaba al jefe también. Un día fui a la sucursal de la ciudad de al lado con él y conseguimos vender unos productos al jefe de la otra empresa.

El último día me dieron un boli como recuerdo de mis prácticas. Fue una experiencia agradable, pero sé que no me gustaría trabajar en una empresa en el futuro.

Juan

Complete the grid **in English**.

(a) place of work		*(1 mark)*
(b) travel and transport		*(1 mark)*
(c) work colleagues		*(1 mark)*
(d) length of experience		*(1 mark)*
(e) tasks done in the office (3)		*(3 marks)*
(f) overall opinion		*(1 mark)*

34 At work

Listen to these young people talking about where they did their work experience.

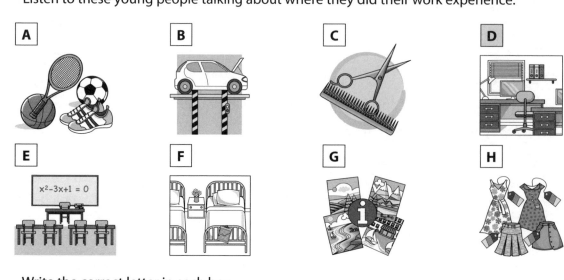

Write the correct letter in each box.

Example: D

1 ☐ *(1 mark)*   **2** ☐ *(1 mark)*   **3** ☐ *(1 mark)*   **4** ☐ *(1 mark)*

Work experience

35 Work experience

Read what these people say about their work experience. Write **P** (positive), **N** (negative) or **P/N** (both positive and negative) in each box.

> Hice un aprendizaje
> – me gustó mucho.
>
> **Ana**

> La semana pasada hice mis prácticas laborales en una papelería. Trabajé muchas horas y fue muy cansado.
>
> **Paco**

> Donde hice mis prácticas laborales, la mayoría de la gente no era maja. Todos estaban muy ocupados. Sin embargo, mi jefe me ayudó bastante.
>
> **Isabel**

> En mis prácticas laborales aprendí mucho, aunque archivar documentos era muy aburrido.
>
> **Ramón**

> En la oficina donde trabajé me trataron muy bien y me gustó mucho.
>
> **Pili**

1 Ana ☐ *(1 mark)*   **4** Ramón ☐ *(1 mark)*

2 Paco ☐ *(1 mark)*   **5** Pili ☐ *(1 mark)*

3 Isabel ☐ *(1 mark)*

36 Carmen's work experience

Listen to Carmen talking about her work experience. Answer the questions **in English**.

(a) What does she say about the timetable?

.... *(1 mark)*

(b) What does she criticise?

.... *(1 mark)*

(c) What did she have to do?

.... *(1 mark)*

(d) What has it made her decide? Name **two** things.

....

.... *(2 marks)*

(e) What does she want to do as a job in the future?

.... *(1 mark)*

Dialogues and messages

37 A telephone message

Part A

Listen to the message. Complete the sentences by writing the correct letter in each box.

Example: San Bernardo school is …

A	unique.
B	specialist.
C	certified.

B

(a) The school is …

A	safe
B	large.
C	tough.

☐ *(1 mark)*

(b) It has the latest …

A	technology.
B	courses.
C	resources.

☐ *(1 mark)*

(c) The teachers have the highest …

A	salaries.
B	expectations.
C	qualifications.

☐ *(1 mark)*

(d) Children leave to 'go forth' and …

A	take part.
B	learn.
C	take a break.

☐ *(1 mark)*

Part B

Which **four** statements are true? Write the correct letters in the boxes.

A	This is a school number.
B	You have to speak to the operator.
C	You can report a pupil absent by pressing number 1.
D	To speak to reception you have to press number 3.
E	You can leave a message.
F	You will have to call back.
G	You have to leave your contact details.
H	Someone will get back to you.

Example: A

☐ ☐ ☐ ☐

(4 marks)

Nouns and articles

> Remember not all words ending in **a** are feminine or ending in **o** are masculine! There are exceptions.

1 Write the correct definite article *el*, *la*, *los*, *las*.

Example: .....la....... gente

1 .... mesa	**6** .... piso
2 .... fútbol	**7** .... ciencias
3 .... patatas fritas	**8** .... guisantes
4 .... dientes	**9** .... problema
5 .... mano	**10** .... foto

2 Complete the sentence with either the definite article *el*, *la*, *los*, *las* or the indefinite article *un*, *una*. Remember to think about gender and whether it is singular or plural.

Example: En casa tengo .....un....... perro que es negro y blanco.

1 En mi opinión, las zanahorias son más ricas que .... judías verdes.

2 En mi casa hay .... cuarto de baño y tres dormitorios.

3 No me gusta nada .... francés porque es complicado.

4 Todos .... martes tengo club de ajedrez.

5 En mi estuche hay .... regla y tres bolígrafos.

6 Mi instituto es grande y hay .... salón de actos.

7 Me he torcido .... tobillo y me duele mucho.

8 .... domingo fuimos a una piscina al aire libre cerca de mi casa.

> Often we use articles in English when in Spanish they are not needed, e.g. talking about jobs, after **sin** and **con**, and after the verb *hablar*.
>
> Sometimes we use articles in Spanish when we would not in English, e.g. talking generally (noun at the start of a sentence), expressing opinions, before the days of the week (*el lunes voy a …*).

3 Read the sentences and cross out any articles that have been used where they are not needed.

Example: No tengo ~~un~~ coche porque prefiero viajar en metro.

1 Vivo en un cómodo bloque de pisos en las afueras.

2 Mi padre es un dentista y mi madre es una enfermera.

3 Hablo el español y el sueco.

4 Escribo con un lápiz en mi clase de matemáticas.

5 El sábado voy a la casa de mis abuelos.

6 El deporte es muy importante para llevar una vida sana.

7 Odio el dibujo porque no puedo dibujar bien.

8 ¿Se puede reservar dos habitaciones con una ducha?

Adjectives

Most adjectives agree as follows:

end in **-e**: add **-s** in the plural

end in **-o**: *alto / alta / altos / altas*

end in **consonant***: add **-es** in the plural

*Nationalities also have a separate feminine singular form: *española*

---

1   Find the correct adjective from the list. Remember that as well as making sense, the adjective must agree with the noun.

Example: una abogada .....*seria*...............

1   una casa ....

2   dos gatos ....

3   un vestido ....

4   las películas son ....

5   el profesor es ....

6   las actrices son ....

7   la playa es ....

8   nuestros coches son ....

adosada
baratos
español
interesantes
preciosa
rojo
seria
simpáticas
traviesos

2   Choose the correct adjective.

Example: Vivo en un apartamento muy *pequeña /(pequeño)/ pequeños*.

1   Me alojé en un hotel *lujoso / lujosa / lujosos* de cuatro estrellas.

2   Me gusta llevar pantalones *cómodas / cómodos / cómodo*.

3   Creo que mi instituto es bastante *bueno / buen / buena*.

4   El paisaje era *impresionantes / impresionante / impresionanto*.

5   La estación de tren está siempre *limpia / limpio / limpias*.

6   Me encantan las ciencias porque son muy *útiles / útil / útilas*.

Some adjectives have shortened forms which are positioned before the noun:

un coche bueno ⟶ *un buen coche*

---

3   Write out these sentences with the correct adjective in the correct place.

Example:

Suelo comer fruta porque es sana y deliciosa. (mucho / mucha)

Suelo comer .....*mucha*............. fruta porque es sana y deliciosa.

1   En Inglaterra hay gente que habla muy bien griego. (poco / poca)

....

2   Lo mejor es que tiene un jardín. (bonito / bonita)

....

3   Estamos porque hace buen tiempo. (contento / contentas)

....

4   En el futuro habrá una estatua aquí en la plaza. (gran / grandes)

....

5   Nuestro apartamento está en el piso. (primera / primer)

....

6   Mis primas son pero viven en Escocia. (alemán / alemanas)

....

Possessives and pronouns

1 Complete the table with the missing possessive adjectives.

English	Spanish singular	Spanish plural
my	mi	
your		tus
his / her / its		
our		nuestros / nuestras
your		
their	su	

2 Complete the phrase with the correct possessive adjective.

  1 My house is big.   .... casa es grande.

  2 His brother is the oldest.   .... hermano es el mayor.

  3 Their sons play tennis.   .... hijos juegan al tenis.

  4 My favourite films are comedies.   .... películas preferidas son las comedias.

  5 Its food is healthy.   .... comida es sana.

Possessive pronouns are like possessive adjectives but replace the noun they describe. They must agree with the noun they replace!

In Spanish they are always accompanied by the definite article:

el mío / la mía, los míos / las mías = mine	*el tuyo / la tuya* = yours
el suyo / la suya = his / hers	*el nuestro / la nuestra* = ours

---

3 Complete these comparisons with the correct possessive pronoun.

  Example: Nuestras toallas son más pequeñas que ...... *las tuyas* .... (yours)
                (Our towels are smaller than yours.)

  1 Tu perro es más feroz que .... (mine)

  2 Mis gafas son menos feas que .... (his)

  3 Tu profe de historia es más callado que .... (ours)

  4 Su abrigo es más cómodo que .... (yours)

4 Rewrite the phrases to create one sentence using the relative pronoun *que*.

  Example: Tengo un hermano. Se llama Diego ⟶ ..... *Tengo un hermano que se llama Diego.* ....

  1 María tiene un gato. Es negro y pequeño.

  ....

  2 Vivimos en un pueblo. Está en el norte de Inglaterra.

  ....

  3 En la clase de literatura tengo que leer un libro. Es muy aburrido.

  ....

Comparisons

To form the comparative:	**más** + adjective + **que** = more … than
	menos + adjective + **que** = less … than
	tan + adjective + **como** = as … as

1 Read the English and then complete the Spanish sentence with the correct comparative adjectives.

Example: My sister is taller than my brother.

Mi hermana es ...... *más alta que* .... mi hermano.

1 My mother is thinner than my father.

Mi madre es .... mi padre.

2 Mariela is less patient than Francisco.

Mariela es .... Francisco.

3 This bus is slower than the train.

Este autobús es .... el tren.

4 Fruit is as healthy as vegetables.

La fruta es .... las verduras.

5 This shirt is as expensive as that jacket.

Esta camisa es .... aquella chaqueta.

Remember!

el / la mejor, los / las mejores = the best

el / la peor, los / las peores = the worst

---

2 Write out the correct superlative sentence.

Example: Esta cafetería es ...... *la menos cara* .... (the least expensive)

1 Mi profesor de inglés es .... (the best)

2 Mis deberes de religión son .... (the worst)

3 Mi mejor amiga es .... de la clase. (the smallest)

4 Sus perros son .... (the most intelligent)

5 Las noticias de Telecinco son .... (the least boring)

| *el / la*
 los / las | + | *más*
 menos | + | adjective | = the most
 = the least |

---

3 Translate these sentences into Spanish.

To translate words like 'incredibly' or 'extremely' don't forget to use the ending *ísimo / a*.

1 My car is the cheapest. ...... *Mi coche es el más barato* ....

2 My cousin is lazier than your uncle. ....

3 Her mobile phone is incredibly small. ....

4 The Spanish exam is extremely easy. ....

5 Horror films are as exciting as action films. ....

6 My school is the ugliest! ....

7 Science is less boring than geography. ....

8 Messi is the best. ....

Other adjectives

> Demonstrative adjectives are used to indicate which thing / person you are referring to ('this', 'those', etc.). There are three in Spanish: one for 'this' / 'these', and two for 'that' / 'those' (to distinguish between 'that' and 'that (further away)'). All forms need to agree in number and gender.

1 Complete the table with the correct demonstrative adjective in the box below.

Masculine singular	Feminine singular	Masculine plural	Feminine plural	Meaning
este				this / these
	esa			that / those
		aquellos		that (over there) / those (over there)

2 Translate into Spanish. (o/t = 'over there')

1 these boots ....
2 this t-shirt ....
3 that girl (o/t) ....
4 those bananas ....
5 that mobile phone ....
6 those magazines (o/t) ....
7 this iPod ....
8 that film ....
9 that train (o/t) ....
10 these hats ....
11 those strawberries ....
12 those boys (o/t) ....

3 Complete the sentence with the correct indefinite adjective in the box below.

cada	todo / toda	algún / alguna
mismo / misma	todos / todas	algunos / algunas
mismos / mismas		

1 Juega al baloncesto .... (every) día.
2 Siempre da la .... (same) opinión.
3 Conozco a .... (some) chicas que trabajan como peluqueras.
4 Ayer, ... (all) los alumnos hicieron sus exámenes.
5 Mi amigo tiene el .... (same) ordenador portátil que yo.

4 Fill in the gaps in the text using both demonstrative and indefinite adjectives. The text is translated for you below.

> El año pasado fui de vacaciones con mi familia. **1** .... los años vamos al sur de Inglaterra, pero este año fuimos a España. **2** .... de mis amigos han ido a España, pero ésta fue mi primera vez. ¡Me gustó mucho! **3** .... los españoles que conocimos eran muy amables y **4** .... hablaban muy bien inglés. En España, a los jóvenes les gusta la **5** .... ropa que a los jóvenes ingleses y nos divierten los **6** .... pasatiempos. ¡Fue muy interesante!

> Last year I went on holiday with my family. Every year we go to the South of England but this year we went to Spain. Some of my friends have been to Spain but this was my first time. I liked it a lot! All the Spanish people we met were really nice and some spoke very good English. In Spain, young people love the same clothes as English young people and we like the same hobbies. It was really interesting!

Pronouns

1 Complete the table with the correct pronouns in English or Spanish.

yo	
	you singular
	he
ella	

	we (masc.)
nosotras	
vosotros	
	you plural (fem.)
ellos	
	they (fem.)

A pronoun replaces a noun. An object pronoun has the action (shown by the verb) done to it. It can be direct or indirect.

She sent it to me.   **it** = direct object, **me** = indirect object

Direct object pronouns: ***me, te, lo / la, nos, os, los / las***

Position of the object pronouns:
* Before a conjugated verb: *lo compro* (I buy it), *lo he comprado* (I have bought it)
* After a negative: *no lo compro* (I don't buy it)
* At the end of an infinitive or gerund (or before the verb): *voy a comprarlo / lo voy a comprar* (I am going to buy it), *estoy comprándolo / lo estoy comprando* (I am buying it)

---

2 Replace the noun with the correct object pronoun.

Example: Miguel ha perdido la maleta. ⟶ ....Miguel la ha perdido.....

1 Hemos perdido las llaves. ....

2 Han perdido la moto. ....

3 Teresa come el bocadillo. ....

4 Compro el vestido. ....

5 No bebo limonada. ....

6 No lavo la ropa. ....

7 Quiero escribir un correo electrónico. ....

8 No quiero leer esa novela. ....

9 Necesito la información ahora. ....

10 Vamos a vender la casa. ....

> **Remember!** You only need to replace the noun. The verb will stay the same.

3 Translate these sentences, which use direct and indirect object pronouns, into English or Spanish.

Example: Le di mi cuaderno de matemáticas. ⟶ .....I gave him my Maths exercise book.....

> Indirect object pronouns: **me, te, le, nos, os, les**

1 Le voy a llamar esta tarde. ....

2 Les visité ayer. ....

3 Lo haré si tengo tiempo. ....

4 Los vendo en el mercado. ....

5 ¿Las has visto? ....

6 She came to visit me at home. ....

7 They sent me the reservation. ....

8 I am going to buy them online. ....

The present tense

To form the present tense, replace the infinitive ending with:

-ar verbs: *o, as, a, amos, áis, an*

-er verbs: *o, es, e, emos, éis, en*

-ir verbs: *o, es, e, imos, ís, en*

Tú is used for people you know and in the present tense will always end in *s*.

Usted is the formal word for you and takes the same ending as *él* or *ella*, and therefore has no *s* at the end.

1 Write the verb in the correct person.

Example: escuchar (tú) → ......*escuchas*......

1 vivir (nosotros) → ....

2 bailar (ellas) → ....

3 vender (yo) → ....

4 llevar (vosotros) → ....

5 odiar (tú) → ....

6 comer (él) → ....

7 salir (nosotros) → ....

8 escuchar (usted) → ....

2 Choose the correct verb for each phrase.

Example: En mi tiempo libre (practico)/ practican deportes.

1 Mis padres *comemos / comen* mucha carne.

2 Mi hermana y yo *vive / vivimos* en un barrio precioso.

3 ¿A qué hora *tienes / tienen* tu clase de natación?

4 Nunca *habla / hablan* en francés porque son tímidos.

5 Usted *debes / debe* firmar aquí.

6 Nuestro amigo es paciente y nunca *grita / gritáis*.

7 Normalmente *chateas / chateo* con mis amigos por Internet.

8 A veces su profesor *lee / leen* en clase.

9 ¿Usted qué *piensa / pensáis* del precio de la gasolina?

10 *Puedes / Podéis* comprar vuestros billetes aquí.

In the present tense, **er** and **ir** verbs are only different for the *nosotros* and *vosotros* parts of the verb and so there are fewer endings to learn!

3 Write the correct part of the verb in each sentence. Watch out for stem changing verbs!

Example: Mis amigos .....*estudian*..... inglés, francés y español. (estudiar)

1 Nos gusta la comida italiana y esta noche .... pizza. (cenar)

2 Los mecánicos a veces .... al aire libre. (trabajar)

3 Me levanto temprano y .... a las ocho y media. (desayunar)

4 Limpia su dormitorio y luego .... la mesa. (poner)

5 Nunca comemos caramelos, pero .... pasteles a menudo. (comprar)

6 ¿Cuánto .... las cebollas? (costar)

7 .... un cartón de leche, pero no tengo dinero. (querer)

8 Los niños .... mucho hoy en día. (pedir)

Reflexives and irregulars

1 Write the correct reflexive pronoun next to each part of the verbs *afeitarse* and *vestirse*.

	afeito
te	afeitas
	afeita
	afeitamos
	afeitáis
se	afeitan

	visto
	vistes
	viste
	vestimos
	vestís
	visten

2 Complete the sentence with the correct reflexive pronoun.

Example: A veces mis amigos no .....se....... lavan.

1 Normalmente, los sábados .... levanta a las nueve y media.

2 Mis amigos no .... peinan, pero yo me peino siempre.

3 ¿A qué hora .... despiertas los domingos?

4 Los profesores .... quejan mucho de sus alumnos.

5 Mis primos .... llaman John y Emma.

6 .... levantamos temprano para ir de vacaciones.

7 ¿............... ducháis por la mañana o por la tarde?

8 .... lavas y te vistes antes de ir al colegio.

3 Rewrite the story for Olivia. Change all the verbs in the 'I' form to the 'she' form. Don't forget to change the non-reflexive verbs, too!

Todos los días me levanto temprano para ir a trabajar. Trabajo en una tienda de ropa famosa. Primero me lavo los dientes y luego me ducho y me visto. Bajo las escaleras y desayuno cereales con fruta. Siempre me peino en la cocina. Después, me lavo la cara en el cuarto de baño que está abajo, al lado de la cocina. Me pongo la chaqueta y salgo a las ocho y media porque el autobús llega a las nueve menos cuarto. Vuelvo a casa a las siete de la tarde.

Todos los días Olivia se levanta

Remember! Some verbs are regular but have an irregular ending in the first person singular. *Poner* is one of those verbs: *pongo, pones, pone,* etc. It can be reflexive when it means putting on clothes. Watch out for *salir,* too – the first person is *salgo.*

Ser and *estar*

> **ser:** use for permanent things (e.g. nationality, occupation, colour, size, personality)
>
> **estar:** use for temporary things (e.g. illness, appearance, feelings) and location

1 Write the correct form of the verb *ser* or *estar*.

Example: .....Somos............. ingleses y vivimos en Londres. (ser – nosotros)

1 ¿Dónde .... el banco? (estar – objeto él / ella)

2 Mis abuelas .... muy generosas. (ser – ellos / ellas)

3 .... de Madrid, pero trabajo en Barcelona. (ser – yo)

4 El vestido .... verde con flores blancas. (ser – objeto)

5 .... las cuatro y media de la tarde. (ser – ellos / ellas)

6 El armario .... enfrente de la puerta. (estar – objeto él / ella)

7 .... muy tristes hoy porque las vacaciones han terminado. (estar – vosotros)

8 .... listos para el examen de teatro. (estar – nosotros)

2 Now translate the sentences from Exercise 1 into English. In brackets, write down the reason why the verb is *ser* or *estar*.

Example: .....We are English and we live in London. ("ser" for nationalities)......

1 ....

2 ....

3 ....

4 ....

5 ....

6 ....

7 ....

8 ....

3 Tick the phrases which use the correct verb 'to be'. Correct those which are wrong.

Example: Estoy en Francia de vacaciones. ✓

La plaza es a mano izquierda. ✗ .....La plaza está a mano izquierda..........

1 Somos británicos y hablamos inglés.

....

2 Mi amigo está inteligente y tiene el pelo negro.

....

3 Me duele la cabeza y soy enfermo.

....

4 Mi perro ha muerto y estoy muy triste.

....

5 Su primo es italiano y trabaja como diseñador.

....

6 Mi madre está dependienta y mi padre está ingeniero.

....

7 Creo que hoy, después de ir a la peluquería, estoy guapa.

....

8 Mi casa está bastante pequeña, tiene solo un dormitorio.

....

The gerund

> Gerunds are –ing words (playing, singing, etc.). To form them replace the infinitive endings as follows: *hablar – hablando, comer – comiendo, vivir – viviendo.*
>
> Remember! Some verbs have irregular gerunds:
> *caer → cayendo*   *oír → oyendo*   *poder → pudiendo*
>
> Some stem-changing **ir** verbs also change their stem in the gerund:
> *pedir → pidiendo*   *dormir → durmiendo*

1 Change the following infinitives into the gerund, and write their meanings in English.

Example: beber → ....bebiendo – drinking............

1 comer → ....
2 saltar → ....
3 correr → ....
4 tomar → ....
5 dormir → ....

6 asistir → ....
7 escribir → ....
8 escuchar → ....
9 aprender → ....
10 poder → ....

2 What are these people doing? Write sentences using the words from the box.

comer pizza	nadar en la piscina	tocar la guitarra
hablar con amigos	escuchar música	ver una película
navegar por Internet	escribir una postal	montar en bicicleta

Example: (he) ....Está nadando en la piscina................

1 (she) ....
2 (I) ....
3 (they) ....
4 (we) ....
5 (you) ....

> The imperfect continuous is formed using the imperfect tense of **estar** + the gerund:
> *estaba comiendo* – I was eating
>
> **estar** in the imperfect tense: *estaba, estabas, estaba, estábamos, estabais, estaban*

3 Translate the first part of the missing sentences into Spanish.

Example: (I was fishing) ....Estaba pescando.................... cuando me caí al agua.

1 (he was sailing) .... cuando llegó la tormenta.
2 (they were eating) .... cuando su madre les llamó.
3 (we were sunbathing) .... cuando empezó a llover.
4 (you were singing) .... cuando salió el tren.
5 (we were watching TV) .... cuando nuestro padre volvió a casa.
6 (I was playing video games) .... cuando llamó.
7 (you were all listening to the teacher) .... cuando entró el perro.
8 (she was swimming in the sea) .... cuando el tiburón apareció.

The preterite tense

> The preterite tense is used to describe completed actions in the past. Replace the infinitive ending with:
>
> **-ar** verbs: *é, aste, ó, amos, asteis, aron*
>
> **-er** and **-ir** verbs: *í, iste, ió, imos, isteis, ieron*
>
> **Remember!** There are lots of irregular verbs in the preterite.
>
> Some have irregular spellings in the first person: *saqué, toqué, crucé, empecé, llegué, jugué*
> The most common irregular verbs are: *ir, ser, hacer, dar, decir, estar* and *tener.*

1 Write the correct verb in the preterite.

Example: comer (tú) ⟶ .....*comiste*...............

   1 sacar (ellos) ⟶ ....

   2 volver (nosotros) ⟶ ....

   3 comprar (él) ⟶ ....

   4 llegar (tú) ⟶ ....

   5 trabajar (vosotros) ⟶ ....

   6 ir (usted) ⟶ ....

   7 dar (yo) ⟶ ....

   8 tener (nosotros) ⟶ ....

   9 visitar (ellas) ⟶ ....

  10 beber (él) ⟶ ....

2 Complete the sentences with the correct verb in the preterite. All these sentences use irregular verbs.

   1 La semana pasada .... (ir) a casa de mis amigos.

   2 Mi novio y yo no .... (tener) tiempo para visitar el museo.

   3 Sus padres nos .... (dar) unos regalos bonitos.

   4 Conchita .... (ir) a la playa con su hermano.

   5 Ayer me .... (levantarse) y .... (vestirse) antes de las nueve.

   6 El lunes mis padres .... (hacer) alpinismo en los Pirineos.

   7 "No es verdad", ... (decir) el niño.

   8 El concierto .... (ser) impresionante. Me gustó mucho.

   9 .... (hacer) mis deberes antes de jugar al fútbol.

  10 Anoche .... (tener) que poner y quitar la mesa y luego salí con mis amigos.

3 Read the text in the present tense and rewrite the text, changing all the verbs in bold into the preterite.

Voy al cine con mis amigos y **vemos** una película de acción. Después **comemos** en un restaurante italiano. **Como** una pizza con jamón y queso, y mi amiga Lola **come** pollo con pasta. **Bebemos** zumo de manzana y mi amigo Tom **come** tarta de chocolate pero yo no **como** postre. Después del restaurante **voy** en tren a casa de mi prima. El viaje **es** largo y aburrido. **Vuelvo** a casa y **me acuesto** a las once de la noche.

.......*Fui al cine con mis amigos y*...

....

....

....

....

....

....

....

The imperfect tense

> Remember! The imperfect is used:
> * to describe repeated actions in the past
> * when you would say 'used to' in English
> * to describe background details.
>
> Replace the infinitive ending with:
>
> **-ar** verbs: **aba**, **abas**, **aba**, **ábamos**, **abais**, **aban**
>
> **-er** and **-ir** verbs: **ía**, **ías**, **ía**, **íamos**, **íais**, **ían**

1 Tick the sentences which contain imperfect verbs and underline the verbs.

Example: Antes mi colegio ....era................. más pequeño. ✓

  1 El miércoles fuimos a la piscina y nadamos durante una hora y media.

  2 De pequeños nadábamos en el mar todas las semanas.

  3 Había mucha gente en el museo y las estatuas eran preciosas.

  4 Mi padre nos preparó una cena vegetariana.

  5 Cuando eran pequeños, no comían tomate ni lechuga.

  6 Gabriela llegó a Madrid en tren para empezar su nuevo trabajo.

  7 Ayer nos encontramos en la cafetería y hablamos toda la tarde.

  8 Me ponía nervioso cada vez que hacía una prueba de vocabulario.

  9 Lo pasé genial porque hizo sol y no llovió.

10 Nevaba todos los días y hacía un frío horrible.

2 Translate the sentences from Exercise 1 into English. Explain your choice of tense in brackets.

Example: ...... My school used to be very small. (imperfect for "used to") ....

  1 ....

  2 ....

  3 ....

  4 ....

  5 ....

  6 ....

  7 ....

  8 ....

  9 ....

10 ....

3 Complete the sentences with the correct verb in the past tense. It could be either the preterite or the imperfect.

Example: El sábado .....fuimos............. a la discoteca a bailar y a divertirnos. (ir)

  1 Cuando mi hermana ....tres años empezó a tocar el piano. (tener)

  2 Mi familia ....en el campo, pero ahora tiene un piso en Londres. (vivir)

  3 ....lloviendo cuando llegamos al camping. (estar)

  4 La semana pasada ....la aspiradora y planché la ropa. (pasar)

  5 Todos los días ....en el jardín y plantaban muchas rosas. (trabajar)

  6 Hizo compras por Internet y ....mucho dinero. (gastar)

  7 Siempre ....fruta y bebíamos mucha agua para estar en forma. (comer)

  8 Una vez ....al tenis con mi profesor de inglés, pero no gané. (jugar)

The future tense

> The **near future** tense is used to say what's going to happen. It is formed using the present tense of *ir* + *a* + an infinitive: *Voy a salir a las dos*. I'm going to go out at two.
>
> Present tense of *ir*: *voy, vas, va, vamos, vais, van*

1 Complete the phrases with the missing parts of the near future tense.

Example: I am going to buy a dress. *Voy .....a.......... comprar un vestido.*

1 We are going to play basketball. *Vamos a .... al baloncesto.*

2 She is going to lay the table. .... *a poner la mesa.*

3 They are going to eat lamb chops. *Van .... comer chuletas de cordero.*

4 I am not going to cry. *No .... a llorar.*

5 Are you going to watch the film? ¿ .... *a ver la película?*

6 You (all) are going to listen and repeat. .... *a escuchar y a repetir.*

7 My mother is going to catch the bus. *Mi madre .... a coger el autobús.*

8 My friends are going to go to Scotland. *Mis amigos van a .... a Escocia.*

9 We are not going to work Saturdays. *No .... a trabajar los sábados.*

10 I am going to go out with my girlfriend. .... *a salir con mi novia.*

> The **future tense** is used to talk about what you will do or what will happen in the future. The future is tense is formed by adding these endings onto the infinitive:
> *-é, -ás, -á, -emos, -éis, -án*
>
> Don't forget the accents!
>
> Remember there are some irregular future verbs: *saldré, diré, tendré, haré,* etc.

2 Write the Spanish for these future sentences. Remember to use the future tense when describing what will happen.

Example: I will buy a dress. *Compraré un vestido.*

1 We are going to watch the film. ....

2 I will not work on Mondays. ....

3 They are going to catch the underground. ....

4 He will go to England. ....

5 They are going to play with my brother. ....

6 You will go to Spain. ....

3 Complete the text with the correct verbs in the near future tense.

| seguir | ser | trabajar | tener | ir | tomar(se) | ser | vivir | ir |

El año que viene mi amiga **1** .... a la universidad a estudiar Biología. Yo no

2 .... a la universidad porque me **3** .... un año sabático. Quiero

trabajar como voluntaria, pero **4** .... que vivir con mis padres para ahorrar dinero.

5 .... como voluntaria para una asociación benéfica que cuida a los sin techo.

6 .... muy interesante, pero me imagino que el trabajo

7 .... muy duro también. Mi hermana **8** .... estudiando en el cole y

mi hermano **9** .... en el extranjero.

The conditional

The conditional is used to describe what you would do or what would happen in the future. To form the conditional, you add the following endings to **the infinitive**:

ía, ías, ía, íamos, íais, ían

All verbs use the same endings, but some verbs don't use the infinitive as the stem. These irregular verbs use the same stem as for the future tense.

1 Remember that the conditional is similar to the future tense and adds its endings on to the infinitive. It also has the same irregulars!

Change these future verbs into the conditional. Write the English for each.

Example: haré ⟶ ....*haría – I would do*.....

1 compraremos ⟶ ....   5 jugarás ⟶ ....

2 saldrán ⟶ ....   6 vendremos ⟶ ....

3 trabajaréis ⟶ ....   7 podrás ⟶ ....

4 estará ⟶ ....   8 habrá ⟶ ....

2 In an ideal world what would happen next year? Create sentences using the conditional.

Example: Mi madre .....*compraría*.............. un perro.

1 Mi profesor .... de vacaciones.	malgastar (= to squander)
2 Nuestros primos .... el sol en la playa.	ir
3 El jefe no .... todos los días.	ganar
4 Mis amigos y yo .... la lotería.	haber
5 No .... contaminación atmosférica.	compartir
6 Más gente .... el transporte público.	comprar
7 Las empresas no .... el agua.	trabajar
8 Los gobiernos .... contra la pobreza mundial.	usar
9 Mi equipo de fútbol .... la liga nacional.	luchar
10 Mi hermano y yo no .... el dormitorio.	tomar / ganar

3 Give advice using the conditional of *deber* or *poder* to help these people.

Example: Tengo dolor de cabeza.

.....*Deberías / Podrías tomar estas pastillas*.......

1 No puedo dormir.

....

tomar estas pastillas
acostarte temprano
comer más fruta y verduras
comprar ropa de segunda mano
consumir menos energía
ir al médico
ir al dentista
hacer más ejercicio
evitar el estrés

2 Como demasiado chocolate.

....

3 No tengo energía.

....

4 Estoy enfermo. ....

5 Estoy cansado todo el tiempo. ....

6 Me duelen las muelas. ....

7 Quiero reducir la contaminación. ....

8 Debo gastar menos dinero. ....

Perfect and pluperfect

> The perfect tense is used to talk about what someone **has done** or what **has happened**, the pluperfect about what someone **had done** or what **had happened**.
>
> Perfect: present tense of **haber** + a past participle.
>
> Pluperfect: imperfect tense of **haber** + a past participle.
>
> To form the past participle replace the infinitive ending with:
> **-ar** verbs: **ado**
> **-er** and **-ir** verbs: **ido**

1   Complete the table with the correct parts of the verb *haber*.

	Perfect tense (I have … etc.)	Pluperfect tense (I had … etc.)	+ past participles (spoken, eaten, lived, etc.)
yo	he		
tú			
él / ella / usted		había	hablado
nosotros / nosotras	hemos		comido
vosotros /vosotras			vivido
ellos / ellas / ustedes		habían	

2   Translate these phrases into English or Spanish. The box below will help you.

Example: He hablado con él. ....I have spoken to him...

1   Hemos perdido el coche. ....

2   ¿Has estudiado español? ....

3   Han comprado un ordenador portátil. ....

4   He hecho mis deberes. ....

5   Hemos visto un documental muy informativo. ....

6   I have broken my arm. ....

7   They have lost their suitcase. ....

8   We have eaten lots of sweets. ....

9   Have you visited the museum today? ....

10   The shop assistant has opened the shop. ....

> Irregular past participles!
>
> | | | | |
> |---|---|---|---|
> | abrir → abierto | escribir → escrito | poner → puesto | ver → visto |
> | decir → dicho | hacer → hecho | romper → roto | volver → vuelto |

3   Change the verbs into the pluperfect to tell the story.

Esta mañana ha sido horrible. 1 .....Había desayunado.......... (desayunar) ya cuando sonó mi móvil. Mi amiga 2 .... (perder) la bolsa en el polideportivo y no tenía dinero suficiente para pagar la entrada. Ella 3 .... (nadar) en la piscina y también 4 .... (ir) a una clase de aerobic. Así que fui al polideportivo para ayudar a mi amiga, pero yo me 5 .... (dejar) la bici en el cole y por eso cogí el autobús. El viaje duró mucho y cuando llegué, mi amiga ya 6 .... (encontrar) su bolsa y su dinero. ¡Qué desastre!

Giving instructions

To give commands:

* to one person (**tú**): use the 'you' singular form of the present tense, minus the final **s**: ¡Escucha! Listen! ¡Abre! Open!

* to more than one person (**vosotros**): change the final **r** of the infinitive to **d**: ¡Escuchad! Listen! ¡Abrid! Open!

Irregular *tú / vosotros* commands include:

	decir	hacer	ir	oír	poner	salir	tener	venir
English	say	make / do	go	hear	put	leave	have	come
tú	di	haz	ve	oye	pon	sal	ten	ven
vosotros	decid	haced	id	oíd	poned	salid	tened	venid

1 Change the following infinitives into familiar singular commands (*tú*). Be careful, some are irregular in command form.

   Example: Hablar más ⟶ ......Habla más........

   1 Doblar a la derecha ⟶ ....

   2 Cruzar la plaza ⟶ ....

   3 Pasar el puente ⟶ ....

   4 Tener cuidado ⟶ ....

   5 Venir aquí ⟶ ....

   6 Cantar más bajo ⟶ ....

   7 Leer en voz alta ⟶ ....

   8 Escuchar bien ⟶ ....

   9 Poner la mesa ⟶ ....

   10 Hacer este ejercicio ⟶ ....

2 Now change the above commands into familiar plural ones (*vosotros*). Remember, to form the *vosotros* commands, you change the *r* of the infinitive to *d*.

   Example: Habla más. ⟶ ......Hablad más...

   1 ....

   2 ....

   3 ....

   4 ....

   5 ....

   6 ....

   7 ....

   8 ....

   9 ....

   10 ....

3 Translate these sentences into Spanish, using either *tú* or *vosotros* commands.

   Example: Listen now! (vosotros) ⟶ ......¡Escuchad ahora!.......

   1 Download the music! (tú) ....

   2 Turn left! (vosotros) ....

   3 Clear the table! (tú) ....

   4 Make the bed! (tú) ....

   5 Do the hovering! (vosotros) ....

The present subjunctive

The subjunctive is used in a range of contexts, e.g.

- to express doubt or uncertainty: *No creo que venga.* I don't think he's coming.

- to express a wish with **querer que**: *Quiero que te calles.* I wish you'd be quiet.

- after **cuando** with the future: *Cuando llegue, le contestaré.* When he arrives, I'll ask him.

- after **ojalá**: *Ojalá haga sol.* Let's hope it's sunny.

- to express a negative opinion: *No es verdad que sea tímida.* It's not true that she's shy.

- to give negative *tú* commands.

The subjunctive is formed by replacing the **-o** ending of the present tense 'I' form with:

-ar verbs: **e, es, e, emos, éis, en**

-er and **–ir** verbs: **a, as, a, amos, áis, an**

Therefore verbs which are irregular in the first person in the present are irregular in the present subjunctive.

ir and **ser** have irregular stems: **vay-** *(ir)* and **se-** *(ser).* The endings are the same.

1 Change these verbs from the present indicative into the present subjunctive.

Example: tenemos → .....*tengamos*.....

1 habla → ....
2 comen → ....
3 voy → ....
4 vives → ....
5 trabajáis → ....

6 sale → ....
7 puede → ....
8 hacen → ....
9 encuentro → ....
10 somos → ....

2 Use the present subjunctive to make these positive *tú* commands into negative ones.

Example: Habla con él. → .....*No hables con él.*.....

1 Come este pastel. → ....
2 Compra aquel vestido. → ....
3 Toma estas pastillas. → ....
4 Bebe un vaso de zumo de naranja. → ....
5 Ve esta película romántica. → ....
6 Firma aquí. → ....
7 Rellena el formulario. → ....
8 Salta tres veces. → ....

3 Complete these sentences with the correct verb in the present subjunctive.

Example: Ojalá mi amiga .....*venga*..... (venir) a visitarme.

1 No creo que los jóvenes .... (trabajar) tanto.
2 No es cierto que .... (hacer) buen tiempo el fin de semana.
3 Ojalá nosotros .... (tener) suerte con los exámenes.
4 No creo que mis profesores .... (ser) estrictos.
5 Cuando .... (ir) a España, compraré un sombrero.
6 Dudo que los adolescentes .... (comprar) CDs.

Negatives

> To make a sentence negative, use **no** in front of the whole verb:
>
> *No me gusta la música jazz.*   I don't like jazz music.
> *No vamos a visitar el palacio.*   We are not going to visit the palace.

1 Write these sentences in the negative.

Example: Tengo clase hoy a las diez. → *No tengo clase hoy a las diez.*

    1 Estudio geografía. → ....

    2 Vamos a las afueras. → ....

    3 Ricardo compró una moto nueva. → ....

    4 Sus padres vieron la tele. → ....

    5 Voy a ir a Francia la semana que viene. → ....

2 Match the English and Spanish.

    1 no … ni … ni …   **a** never

    2 no … nada   **b** not … either

    3 no … tampoco   **c** no / not any

    4 no … nadie   **d** nothing / not anything

    5 no … jamás   **e** not … (either) … or …

    6 no … nunca   **f** never

    7 no … ningún/ninguna   **g** no one

3 Rewrite the sentence with the negative words.

    Example: Mateo habla mucho de sus vacaciones. (no, nunca)

        Mateo no habla nunca de sus vacaciones.

> Note that *ninguno* must agree with the noun it precedes: *ninguna ropa* (no clothes)

    1 Mis profesores enseñan cómo teclear. (no, nunca) ....

    2 En mi casa tuvimos una sala de juegos. (no, jamás) ....

    3 Me he quemado los brazos. (no, nunca) ....

    4 Aquí tengo vestidos, faldas y camisetas. (no, ni, ni, ni) ....

    5 Vas a comprar un coche. (no, ningún) ....

    6 Mis padres escuchan. (no, a nadie) ....

3 Translate the sentences into Spanish. Be careful with the word order.

    Example: He never plays football when it rains.

        Nunca juega al fútbol cuando llueve. / No juega nunca al fútbol cuando llueve.

    1 In the afternoon we never drink coffee. ....

    2 I don't iron, cook or clean. ....

    3 They do not speak any languages. ....

    4 We can't talk to anybody during the exam. ....

        ....

    5 I will never smoke because it is a waste of time. ....

        ....

Special verbs

A few verbs like **gustar** are generally used in the 3rd person with a pronoun:
Me gusta bailar. I like dancing.

If the thing that is liked is plural, you use **me gustan**: Me gustan los perros. I like dogs.

encantar, doler, apetecer and *hacer falta* behave in the same way:
Le duele la garganta. His throat hurts.
Me hacen falta dos vasos. I need two glasses.

1 Complete the table with the correct pronouns.

me		I like
	gusta (sing.)	you like
	gustan (pl.)	he / she / it likes

		we like
	gusta (sing.)	you (all) like
	gustan (pl.)	they like

2 Tick the sentences which use the impersonal verb correctly. Correct the other sentences.

Remember! If the impersonal verb is followed by an infinitive, the singular form is always used:
*Les **gusta** tocar la guitarra.* = They like to play the guitar.
You need to use *a* with a proper name: *A Paz le gusta correr.* Paz likes to run.

Example: Me gusta mucho los idiomas y por eso quiero viajar más. ✗

.......*Me gustan mucho los idiomas y por eso quiero viajar más.*......

1 A Pilar y a Pablo les interesan los ordenadores y la informática.

....

2 Nos apetecen ir al teatro mañana.

....

3 Es verdad que le duelen mucho las muelas.

....

4 No nos gustan la contaminación atmosférica.

....

5 ¿Te hace falta unas toallas?

....

3 Unjumble the words to make sentences using an impersonal verb.

Example: gustan / las / me / zanahorias / mucho .....*Me gustan mucho las zanahorias.*.....

1 falta / abrigo / nos / un / hace ....

2 os / caballos / encantan / los / negros ....

3 María / le / aquellos / zapatos / a / gustan ....

4 quedan / veinte / te / euros / regalo / comprar / para / el

....

5 todo / me / el / la / garganta / tiempo / duele

....

6 encantan / rascacielos / porque / les / son / modernos / los

....

Por and *para*

> Remember that **por** and **para** don't just mean 'for'. They can be translated in various ways depending on the sentence. For example: in, in order to, per, instead of, etc.

1 Translate these sentences, which use *para*, into English.

   1 Para mi cumpleaños quiero un móvil nuevo.

   ....

   2 Mi amiga trabaja para un abogado.

   ....

   3 Las aplicaciones para iPhone son increíbles.

   ....

   4 Como muchas verduras y pescado para estar en forma.

   ....

   5 Necesitas la llave para entrar en casa.

   ....

   6 Fumar es muy malo para la salud.

   ....

   7 Van a organizar una fiesta para celebrar el fin de curso.

   ....

   8 Para mí, los deportes son siempre divertidos.

   ....

2 Rewrite the sentences with the word *por* in the correct place.

   Example: Muchas gracias los pantalones. ...... *Muchas gracias por los pantalones.* ......

   1 El coche rojo pasó las calles antiguas.

   ....

   2 Normalmente la mañana me gusta desayunar cereales y fruta.

   ....

   3 Mandé la reserva correo electrónico.

   ....

   4 Me gustaría cambiar este jersey otro.

   ....

   5 En la tienda ganamos diez euros hora.

   ....

   6 Había mucha basura todas partes.

   ....

3 Complete the sentence with either *por* or *para*.

   Example: ..... *Por* .... la tarde prefiero descansar.

   1 .... perder peso, lo más importante es beber mucha agua.

   2 Mis amigas compraron unas flores .... la profesora.

   3 Tengo que cambiar este diccionario .... otro.

   4 Hemos reservado una habitación .... tres noches.

   5 Los alumnos tienen que completar los ejercicios .... el lunes.

Questions and exclamations

Don't forget that Spanish question words have accents. Questions and exclamations have an inverted question mark (¿) or exclamation mark (¡) at the beginning.

1 Use the question words in the box to complete the table below.

¿Qué?	¿Cuánto?	¿Dónde?	¿Cuándo?	¿Cuáles?
¿Adónde?	¿Por qué?	¿Cuántos?	¿Cómo?	¿Cuál?

1	Why?	
2	What?	¿Qué?
3	When?	
4	How?	
5	Where?	
6	Where to?	
7	Which?	¿Cuál?
8	Which ones?	
9	How much?	
10	How many?	

2 Match the Spanish and the English for these exclamations. Write the correct letters in the grid.

1	¡Qué lástima!	**A**	What a problem!
2	¡Qué va!	**B**	How strange!
3	¡Qué rollo!	**C**	How cool!
4	¡Qué difícil!	**D**	How terrible!
5	¡Qué problema!	**E**	No way!
6	¡Qué guay!	**F**	What a shame!
7	¡Qué bien!	**G**	How boring!
8	¡Qué raro!	**H**	How embarrassing!
9	¡Qué vergüenza!	**I**	Great!
10	¡Qué horror!	**J**	How difficult!

1	2	3	4	5	6	7	8	9	10
F									

3 Complete the question or exclamation with the appropriate word or phrase.

rollo	guay	por qué	cuánto	dónde	horror

Example: ¿De .....dónde..... son ustedes?

1 Me he roto la pierna. ¡Qué ....!

2 ¿................... cuesta el jamón serrano?

3 ¿................... trabajas, Ramona?

4 Vamos a ir de vacaciones.

   ¡Qué ....!

5 El viaje en autocar va a durar ocho horas.

   ¡Qué ....!

Connectives and adverbs

Not all adverbs end in *-mente*:
bien – well   *siempre* – always   *bastante* – enough   *poco* – a little
mal – badly   *demasiado* – too   *a menudo* – frequently / often

1 Turn these adjectives into adverbs. Remember to make them feminine first!

Example: fácil → *fácilmente*

1 rápido → ....

2 difícil → ....

3 lento → ....

4 alegre → ....

5 tranquilo → ....

2 Match the connectives correctly. Write the correct letter.

1 además de		**A** but
2 y / e		**B** therefore
3 pero		**C** even if
4 sin embargo		**D** also
5 también		**E** and
6 por eso / por lo tanto		**F** if
7 porque		**G** because
8 ya que		**H** then
9 si		**I** or
10 o / u		**J** since
11 aunque		**K** however
12 entonces		**L** as well as

1	2	3	4	5	6	7	8	9	10	11	12
L											

3 Rewrite 1–5 with the correct adverb. Complete 6–8 with the correct connective.

Example: Los alumnos juegan al rugby. (well) *Los alumnos juegan bien al rugby.*

1 Sus padres cantan en la iglesia. (badly)

....

2 No hablo porque soy tímido. (much)

....

3 El tren pasa por el túnel. (quickly)

....

4 Los pendientes son caros. (too)

....

5 Comemos huevos por la mañana. (frequently)

....

6 Vamos a ir a la piscina .... hace buen tiempo.

7 Odio mi instituto .... hay acoso escolar.

8 El piso es muy moderno, ... no tiene lavaplatos.

Remember! Adverbs can go before or after the verb they relate to:
Siempre como carne. / Como siempre carne.

Numbers

1 Write the number.

Example: trece .....13...........

A veinte	**K** diecinueve ....
B cuarenta y ocho	**L** quinientos ....
C nueve	**M** un millón ....
D cien	**N** novecientos ....
E catorce	**O** ochenta y ocho ....
F mil	**P** setenta y seis ....
G trescientos	**Q** sesenta y siete ....
H cincuenta y siete	**R** diez ....
I veintitrés	**S** cero ....
J quince	**T** veintinueve ....

2 Write these dates and years in Spanish.

Example: 4 May .....*el cuatro de mayo*..............

1 1999 ....

2 10 October ....

3 1 January ....

4 3 March ....

5 2013 ....

6 16 November ....

7 30 May ....

8 1968 ....

9 2002 ....

10 21 April ....

> Ordinal numbers (*primero, segundo, tercero*, etc.) are not used for dates, except for *primero* which can be used. Both of these are correct:
> *el uno de diciembre*
> *el primero de diciembre*

3 Write down these prices in words.

Example: 48,50 € .....*cuarenta y ocho euros con cincuenta*...........

1 20,25 € ....

2 59,10 € ....

3 100,75 € ....

4 87 € ....

5 45,20 € ....

6 7,99 € ....

7 86,70 € ....

8 30,65 € ....

Practice Exam Paper: Reading

This Practice Exam Paper has been written to help you practise what you have learned and may not be representative of a real exam paper.

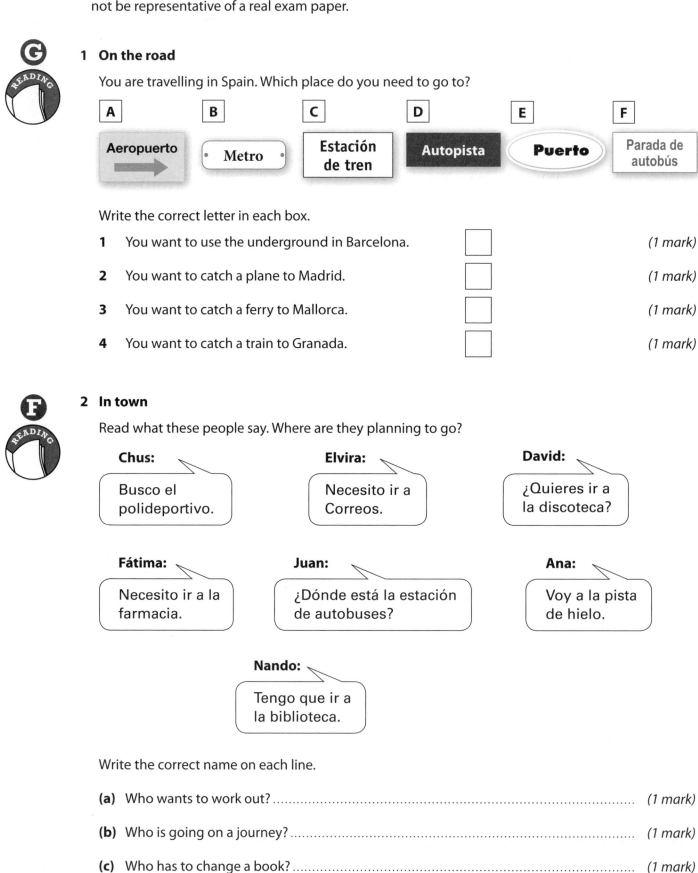

G

1 On the road

You are travelling in Spain. Which place do you need to go to?

A	B	C	D	E	F
Aeropuerto →	Metro	Estación de tren	Autopista	Puerto	Parada de autobús

Write the correct letter in each box.

1   You want to use the underground in Barcelona. ☐ *(1 mark)*

2   You want to catch a plane to Madrid. ☐ *(1 mark)*

3   You want to catch a ferry to Mallorca. ☐ *(1 mark)*

4   You want to catch a train to Granada. ☐ *(1 mark)*

F

2 In town

Read what these people say. Where are they planning to go?

Chus: Busco el polideportivo.

Elvira: Necesito ir a Correos.

David: ¿Quieres ir a la discoteca?

Fátima: Necesito ir a la farmacia.

Juan: ¿Dónde está la estación de autobuses?

Ana: Voy a la pista de hielo.

Nando: Tengo que ir a la biblioteca.

Write the correct name on each line.

(a) Who wants to work out? .... *(1 mark)*

(b) Who is going on a journey? .... *(1 mark)*

(c) Who has to change a book? .... *(1 mark)*

(d) Who needs to buy some stamps? .... *(1 mark)*

(e) Who isn't feeling well? .... *(1 mark)*

3 Blogging

Read the following blog entries about part-time jobs.

> **Título:** Mi trabajo a tiempo parcial
> **Luisa:** Reparto periódicos todos los días.
> **Antonio:** Trabajo en una oficina.
> **Javier:** Me gusta trabajar en un instituto.
> **Mar:** Me encanta trabajar en un restaurante.
> **Ángel:** Trabajo al aire libre con niños.
> **Isabel:** No me gusta nada trabajar en casa.
> **Martín:** Los fines de semana trabajo en una tienda.

Answer the questions. Write the correct name on each line.

(a) Who works in an office? .... *(1 mark)*

(b) Who works from home? .... *(1 mark)*

(c) Who works in a shop? .... *(1 mark)*

(d) Who works in a restaurant? .... *(1 mark)*

(e) Who works outside? .... *(1 mark)*

4 A family holiday

Read this e-mail from Juani about her holidays in Santander.

> ¡Hola!
> 1 Todos los años mi familia y yo pasamos una semana de vacaciones en la ciudad de Santander. Normalmente nos alojamos en un hotel frente al mar. La playa es bastante bonita, pero para mí, el agua está demasiado fría para nadar.
> 2 Muchos turistas vienen a Santander en ferry. La mayoría de los restaurantes tienen buena fama. Muchos quieren comer en uno de los muchos sitios donde sirven pescado y mariscos.
> 3 A mi madre le gusta comprar recuerdos en las tiendas de la ciudad, mientras que mi padre se entretiene mirando los barcos en el puerto. Personalmente, no me gusta el mercado. Es interesante, pero hay demasiados turistas.

Match each paragraph with the correct summary below.

A	Talks about the history of Santander.
B	Talks about the local delicacies to eat.
C	Discusses what Juani and her family like to do there.
D	Describes how to get to Santander.
E	Talks about the resort.
F	Describes the weather while she was there.

Write the correct letter in each box.

(a) Paragraph 1 ☐ *(1 mark)*   **(c)** Paragraph 3 ☐ *(1 mark)*

(b) Paragraph 2 ☐ *(1 mark)*

5 Myself and my family

Read this email from Antonio.

> ¡Hola!
>
> Me llamo Antonio y vivo en Barcelona con mis padres y mis hermanos. Tengo un ordenador y me encanta escribir en blogs y mandar correos electrónicos a mis amigos. Me encantan los deportes y de mayor me gustaría ser futbolista profesional.
>
> Ana, mi novia, es muy generosa y me ayuda con mis deberes cuando me resultan muy difíciles. Los sábados paseamos en bicicleta por el parque porque nos gusta estar al aire libre.
>
> La semana que viene Ana y yo vamos a pasar quince días en casa de su tía. Tiene un piso grande en Sevilla donde viven todos sus primos. ¡Será muy divertido!
>
> ¡Hasta luego!
>
> Antonio

Complete the sentences. Write the correct letter in each box.

(a) Besides blogging, Antonio loves …

A	downloading films.
B	sending emails.
C	surfing the internet.

☐ *(1 mark)*

(b) His girlfriend …

A	loves sport.
B	lends him money.
C	helps him with homework.

☐ *(1 mark)*

(c) They are fond of …

A	team games.
B	outdoor pursuits.
C	going to the gym.

☐ *(1 mark)*

(d) Antonio and Ana are going to …

A	his parents house.
B	Ana's relatives' house.
C	his cousin's house.

☐ *(1 mark)*

6 Sunday trading

Read this article.

Tiendas abiertas los domingos

Antes cerraban las tiendas los fines de semana, pero ya no. El hecho de que estén abiertas a todas horas atrae mucho a jóvenes y a mayores. Hablamos con algunas personas que estaban de compras sobre cuándo suelen ir a las tiendas.

David (16 años) nos contó que, simplemente, no tiene tiempo durante la semana para comprar, así que los nuevos horarios le vienen muy bien.

Celia Gonzales (85 años) dice que la compra es su actividad principal. ¡Lo hace a pesar de su edad y le encanta!

El señor López, jefe de un gran complejo comercial cerca de Madrid, nos habló de las ganancias del domingo anterior. Según él, al mediodía el aparcamiento estaba completamente lleno, las cafeterías no tenían sitio suficiente para su clientela y la gente estaba haciendo muchas compras. Dijo que la mayoría buscaban ropa, sobre todo en las tiendas de moda, aunque también eran populares las tiendas de tecnología y de electrodomésticos. Parece ser que los supermercados obtuvieron muchas ganancias, pero menos que el sábado.

El señor López está convencido de que las tiendas abiertas veinticuatro horas benefician a los dependientes y a los clientes, así que han puesto el letrero de abierto los domingos por la mañana.

Which **four** of these statements are true? Write the correct letters in the boxes.

A	Mrs Gonzales got to the shops at 1 o'clock.
B	The clothes shops were very busy.
C	David only shops at weekends.
D	Fashion items were popular.
E	Shopping has become the most popular hobby.
F	Cafés have trouble attracting customers on Sundays.
G	The car park closed at midday.
H	The shops won't close in the future.

☐ ☐ ☐ ☐

(4 marks)

B

7 Letter to a hotel

Read Juan's letter.

> Londres, 2 de septiembre de 2013
>
> Hotel Buena Vista
>
> Estimado señor:
>
> El pasado mes de agosto pasé quince días en el hotel Buena Vista con mi familia. Nuestra habitación era muy cómoda y el servicio que ofrecieron los camareros en el restaurante fue excelente. Desafortunadamente, la piscina estuvo cerrada dos días, pero disfrutamos también de muchas excursiones a muy buen precio.
>
> Quiero darles las gracias por el servicio tan amable. Su hotel es realmente precioso. Intentaremos volver el año que viene.
>
> Atentamente,
>
> Juan López

Which of the **four** following statements are true? Write the correct letters in the boxes.

A	Juan is writing a letter of complaint.
B	He spent a week at the hotel last month.
C	Their room was comfortable and waiters efficient.
D	The excursions were good value.
E	The excursions were cheap but didn't always take place.
F	They couldn't swim whenever they wanted to.
G	The only drawback was that the hotel was expensive.
H	They'd like to come back next year.

☐ ☐ ☐ ☐

(4 marks)

8 Abel Vázquez Cortijo – Paralympian

Read this article.

> Abel Vázquez empezó a hacer judo influenciado por sus padres principalmente, ya que ellos también fueron deportistas de éxito en su juventud representando a España en la selección.
>
> Es discapacitado, ya que tiene problemas de visión. Tiene dificultad para leer las letras de tamaño pequeño. También le resulta difícil salir de casa, ya que necesita poner gran atención por donde camina.
>
> Todas sus medallas están colocadas en un lugar donde todos puedan verlas, y así comparte su experiencia y motiva a más gente con discapacidades.
>
> Dice que lo más importante es la determinación, la responsabilidad y el entusiasmo para realizar nuestros sueños – sean cuales sean tus circunstancias y problemas.
>
> ¡Es un buen ejemplo a seguir para todos!

Answer the following questions **in English**.

(a) How was Abel influenced to get into judo?

.... *(1 mark)*

(b) What is the nature of his disability?

.... *(1 mark)*

(c) What does the article say he has difficulty doing?

.... *(1 mark)*

(d) How can you tell that Abel is a successful sportsman?

.... *(1 mark)*

(e) What has he done to share his experience with other disabled people?

.... *(1 mark)*

(f) What are the most important qualities to have so that your dreams will come true, according to Abel?

.... *(1 mark)*

> When the questions are in English, always read them carefully first. They will give you clues about the content of the reading text.

9 Problem page

Read these problems and answers.

A

Carmen: No sé qué hacer. La gente siempre intenta convencerme para que haga cosas que no me apetecen. Tengo miedo a decir que no. ¿Qué puedo hacer?

Respuesta: Carmen, no te desesperes. Simplemente tienes que ser fuerte y lista, y dar excusas creíbles cuando algo no te apetezca. Recuerda que a los que son amigos de verdad, les vas a gustar hagas lo que hagas.

B

Gorka: Estoy muy mal porque no tengo dinero para hacer las cosas que quiero. ¿Me puedes dar algún consejo?

Respuesta: Es cuestión de usar tu imaginación, Gorka. Habla con tus amigos para pensar qué cosas podéis hacer por poco dinero.

C

Alba: Estoy muy sola. A pesar de que tengo muchos hermanos, son muy pequeños y donde vivo no tengo amigos de mi edad.

Respuesta: Muy fácil, Alba. Lo mejor es hacerte socia de una organización de tu barrio donde practiquen algún deporte u otra actividad que te guste. Allí harás amigos rápidamente.

D

Ricardo: No sé si me puedes ayudar. Es que estoy muy preocupado porque no sé qué voy a hacer después del colegio. Donde vivo no hay trabajo y no tengo dinero para estudiar en la universidad.

Respuesta: ¡Ante todo no te preocupes! Estudia mucho para sacar buenas notas y haz actividades fuera del colegio. Así tendrás un currículum interesante. El futuro se arreglará solo.

E

Cristiano: ¡Estoy desesperado! Me llevo muy mal con mis padres. Me presionan mucho con los estudios y no me dejan salir con mis amigos. Me tratan como a un niño.

Respuesta: ¡Es imprescindible hablar! Explícales lo que te molesta y escucha sus quejas también. Llega a un acuerdo, todo es cuestión de equilibrio.

Match the correct person with each of the problems listed in the grid below. Write the correct letter for each person. For each problem, note the advice given.

Problem	Person	Advice	
Example: peer pressure	A	Be your own person.	
(a) parents			*(2 marks)*
(b) no money			*(2 marks)*
(c) worried about the future			*(2 marks)*
(d) being lonely			*(2 marks)*

Practice Exam Paper: Listening

This Practice Exam Paper has been written to help you practise what you have learned and may not be representative of a real exam paper.

1 Shops

Listen to these shoppers. Which shop do they need to go to?

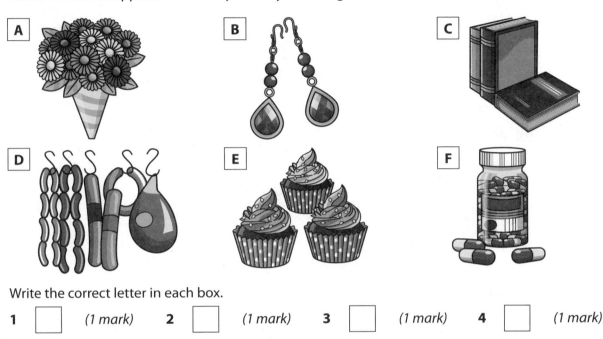

Write the correct letter in each box.

1 ☐ *(1 mark)* **2** ☐ *(1 mark)* **3** ☐ *(1 mark)* **4** ☐ *(1 mark)*

2 A trip to the zoo

Listen to **Conchi**, **David** and **Ana** talking about their recent trip to the zoo.

Who says what? Write the name of the correct person on each line.

Example: Who thinks it was a good day out? ..... David .....

(a) Who mentions the weather? .... *(1 mark)*

(b) Who mentions the food? .... *(1 mark)*

(c) Who thought the journey was too long? .... *(1 mark)*

(d) Who wants to go there again? .... *(1 mark)*

3 My town

Listen to some people talking about their town.

A	where it is	E	the shops
B	the size of the town	F	the weather
C	the activities	G	the activities
D	the transport system	H	the cost of living

Write the letters of the things they mention in the first box and their opinion, **P** (positive) or **N** (negative), in the second.

1 ☐ ☐ *(1 mark)*   **3** ☐ ☐ *(1 mark)*

2 ☐ ☐ *(1 mark)*   **4** ☐ ☐ *(1 mark)*

4 Favourite activities

Listen to some young people talking about their favourite activities. What do they mention?

Write the correct letter in each box.

(a) Gorka likes …

(1 mark)

(b) Andrea likes …

  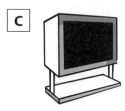

(1 mark)

(c) Marcelo likes …

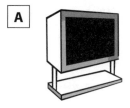  

(1 mark)

(d) Lupe enjoys …

  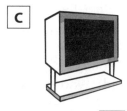

(1 mark)

5 Easy reading

Listen to Lourdes talking about her latest gadget. Which **four** things does she mention?

A	It is heavy.	E	It is expensive but worth the money.
B	It is easy to use.	F	You can make the text bigger.
C	It is the latest model.	G	It isn't suitable for younger readers.
D	It is small.	H	You can download books easily.

Write the **four** correct letters in the boxes.

(4 marks)

116

6 Booking a hotel

Listen to this telephone conversation.

Complete the sentences. Write the correct letter in each box.

(a) The caller wants to book a room for …

A	1 person.
B	3 people.
C	4 people.

☐ *(1 mark)*

(b) On the day she asks about, the hotel …

A	has lots of vacancies.
B	is full.
C	has only one free room.

☐ *(1 mark)*

(c) She wants to stay for …

A	3 nights.
B	4 nights.
C	5 nights.

☐ *(1 mark)*

(d) In the room she wants …

A	twin beds.
B	bunk beds.
C	double beds.

☐ *(1 mark)*

(e) The caller's name is Raquel …

A	Lombarda.
B	Lambada.
C	La Bamba.

☐ *(1 mark)*

7 A new youth club

Listen to an advert for a new youth club. Answer these questions **in English**.

(a) What is happening on the 3rd?

.... *(1 mark)*

(b) What is happening on Tuesday?

.... *(1 mark)*

(c) What facilities are available for keen swimmers? Mention **two** things.

.... *(2 marks)*

(d) What does the advert say about the cost of membership?

.... *(1 mark)*

(e) What will you get for just turning up?

.... *(1 mark)*

(f) What else will be available?

.... *(1 mark)*

8 The internet

Listen to someone talking about internet use. Complete the grids below.

Write your answers **in English.** Full sentences are not required.

Part A

Positive aspects
(a)
(b)
(c)
(d)

(4 marks)

Part B

Negative aspects
(a)
(b)
(c)
(d)

(4 marks)

9 In hospital

Listen to Feliciano talking about his stay in hospital. Answer the questions **in English**.

(a) What happened to Feliciano just after he finished his exams?

.... *(1 mark)*

(b) What injuries did he have?

.... *(1 mark)*

(c) Why doesn't he like being there?

.... *(1 mark)*

(d) What happened to his neighbour?

.... *(1 mark)*

(e) What is his opinion of hospital food?

.... *(1 mark)*

Answers

Lifestyle

1. Birthdays

1   **(a)** March E   **(b)** June D
     (c) July C   **(d)** December B
     (e) October F

2   **1** B   **2** E   **3** F   **4** D

2. Pets

3   **(a)** E   **(b)** B   **(c)** C   **(d)** A

4   **1** N   **2** P/N   **3** P/N   **4** P

3. Physical description

5   D, E, F H

6   **1** J   **2** A   **3** D   **4** F

4. Character description

7   **Part A**: C, D, F, I

    Part B: C, D, F, I,

5. Brothers and sisters

8   **(a)** 14 C   **(b)** younger C
     (c) alike C   **(d)** badly A

9   **1** E   **2** D   **3** A   **4** B

6. Extended family

10   **A** N   **B** P   **C** P+N   **D** N
    E P+N   **F** P   **G** N   **H** P

11   A, C, E, H

7. Friends

12   A, D, F

13   **(a) (i)** He's always helping people.
       (ii) He would do anything for you.
    (b) (i) They always know how to listen to you.
       (ii) They'd never lie to you.
    (c) He never studies at school or does his homework.
    (d) He scored eight goals. / He was named best football player in the school.
    (e) Go to / Be at the football match to support Javier.

8. Daily routine

14   **(a)** At 6:15.
    (b) Jeans.
    (c) On foot / he walked.
    (d) Relax.
    (e) No homework.

15   **(a)** It's boring.
    (b) Because school starts at 8:45.
    (c) Any two of: He showers / He gets dressed / He gets his bag ready.
    (d) He doesn't have breakfast at home. He eats a sandwich or something on his way to school

9. Breakfast

16   A, B, D, E

17   C, E, F, I

10. Eating at home

18   **1** Gustavo P   **2** Isabel P+N
    3 Sofía P+N   **4** Pablo N

19   **1** Dolores D   **2** Paco C
    3 Loli E   **4** Jorge F

11. Eating in a café

20   **1** Elvira – orange juice
    2 Juan – still water
    3 Fátima – ham sandwich
    4 Nando – a vanilla ice cream

21   **1** F   **2** A   **3** B   **4** E

12. Eating in a restaurant

22   **1** C   **2** F   **3** I   **4** D

23   **(a)** A   **(b)** C   **(c)** B   **(d)** A

13. Healthy eating

24   **(a)** C   **(b)** E   **(c)** B   **(d)** D

25   **1** Avelina: Eat less junk food – It contains too much fat.
    2 Alfonso: Eat less salt – Bad for the heart.
    3 Carolina: Cook at home – Easier to eat healthy food / have a balanced diet.
    4 Juan: Eat a more nutritious diet – Stay healthy.

14. Keeping fit and healthy

26   **(a)** Exercise: Need to do it daily.
    Some have a personal trainer but that is not essential.
    Adjust daily routine a little.
    (b) Changes to daily routine: Go to bed earlier.
    Take a short walk when you get up in the morning.
    (c) Stress: Have a positive attitude.
    Talk to someone about your problems.
    (d) Alcohol and smoking: Can drink a little alcohol occasionally.
    Don't smoke at all.

15. Health problems

27 **(a)** Alcoholism among young people.

(b) (i) & (ii) *Any two of*: They drink too much and too quickly in gatherings. / Increase in their alcohol tolerance and consumption of alcohol. / They suffer headaches and memory damage (loss). / They begin to drink in secret.

(c) They should seek help or advice (from parents, teachers or doctors).

(d) (i) Insecurity.
(ii) Paranoia.

(e) (i) & (ii) *Any two of*: aggressive and antisocial behaviour / loss of a job and friends / problems with family and friends.

16. Future relationships

28 **(a)** N   **(b)** A   **(c)** L   **(d)** A
(e) L   **(f)** L   **(g)** N

29 **1** Leonardo would like to meet someone who is <u>nice / kind</u> and thinks that <u>the way you look / appearance</u> is unimportant.

2 Mario would like to meet someone who is <u>funny</u> and thinks <u>money</u> is unimportant.

17. Social issues

30 **(a)** poverty / unemployment

(b) violence / mistreatment, abuse

(c) emigrate

(d) makes them vulnerable / suffer because takes them away from their families / desperation makes them turn to drugs / alcohol

(e) looking for solutions

31 **(a)** Because he had problems when he was young.

(b) Problems at home / with the family / lack of communication (between generations) / young people not getting on with their parents or brothers / sisters.

(c) It (these problems) has (have) been documented / going on for centuries.

(d) (i) Violence.
(ii) Homelessness (being thrown out).

(e) (i) Negotiate / mediate.
(ii) Find housing / a place to stay for the young person.

(f) Separations don't last for long / parties can arrive at an agreement.

18. Social problems

32 **(a)** A   **(b)** C   **(c)** A   **(d)** B

33 **1** B   **2** F   **3** D   **4** A

Leisure

19. Hobbies

1 **(a)** C   **(b)** D   **(c)** F   **(e)** E

2 **1** Marta **D**   **2** Luis **E**   **3** Pablo **B**
4 Cristina **A**

3 **(a)** C   **(b)** B   **(c)** C   **(d)** A

20. Sport

4 E, C, B, A

21. Arranging to go out

5 **(a)** What excuses people give when they turn down an invitation they don't want to accept.

(b) My parents won't let me.

(c) 12 per cent.

(d) Washing your hair. It doesn't take a whole evening to do this.

6 **1** ND   **2** A   **3** A   **4** D

22. Last weekend

7 **(a)** Javier   **(b)** David   **(c)** Luci   **(d)** David

8 **(a)** B   **(b)** A   **(c)** B   **(d)** C

23. TV programmes

9 **1** G   **2** E   **3** A   **4** C

10 **(a)** They are less interesting than cartoons / more boring than cartoons.

(b) Reality TV programmes.

(c) Documentaries.

(d) They don't interest her.

(e) The news.

(f) Because she likes to find out what is going on in the world.

24. Cinema

11 B, D, G, I

12 **(a)** B   **(b)** C   **(c)** C   **(d)** A

25. Music

13 **(a)** Manos   **(b)** Graciela   **(c)** Paco   **(d)** Beatriz

14 **(a)** To study music. / Because he was looking for good opportunities.

(b) (i) It's the best meal of the day.
(ii) He's attracting plenty of fans. / He's on the road to success.

(c) (i) He plays / writes songs.
(ii) He goes out.

(d) He has too many ideas for songs. / His ideas for songs don't let him sleep.

(e) He gives a concert / radio broadcasts.

(f) He talks to promote his music.

26. New technology

15 **(a)** What can you do if you are young and bored?

    (b) *Any two of*: It's fast. / It's easy. / You can do everything from home. / It's convenient.

    (c) It's cheaper. / You can read the reviews before choosing one.

    (d) Even young people need to know what's going on in the world.

    (e) She's started studying French. / She's learning to play the guitar.

27. Internet language

16 **(a)** In the evenings.

    (b) About 4 hours.

    (c) Her own web page.

    (d) It is too complicated.

17 Daniel: **(a)** P   **(b)** P/N   **(c)** P/N

    Ana: **(a)** P+N   **(b)** N   **(c)** P

28. Internet pros and cons

18 **(a)** To talk about internet safety.

    (b) She checked the students' blogs.

    (c) *Any two of*: It's a great method of communication. / It's good for speaking to family and friends. / It's good for buying and selling online.

    (d) Because she had include too many personal details in her blogs.

    (e) She named her school.

    (d) The name and address of the park where she hangs out with her friends. / She uploaded a recent picture of hers that shows her age clearly.

    (e) She has changed lots of information on her web page. / She is more careful about what she writes when she communicates online

29. Shops

19 **(a)** *Any two of*: increase of online shopping / low earnings / cost of rent / cost of parking.

    (b) *Any two of*: cheaper / more convenient / can do this from home.

    (c) *Any two of*: survey local residents / free park and ride schemes / tackle crime

    (d) Contact the help desk.

    (e) Town-centre shopping will disappear forever.

30. Shopping for food

20 **1** B   **2** C   **3** F   **4** A

21 B, C, E, G, H

31. At the market

22 **(a)** B **(b)** E   **(c)** D   **(e)** F

23 **1** Begoña – salad   **2** Pedro – strawberries   **3** Rodrigo – meat   **4** Lucía – vegetables

32. Clothes and colours

24 **(a)** Paco **(b)** Marina **(c)** Juan **(d)** Patri

33. Shopping for clothes

25 **1** E **2** C   **3** B   **4** A

26 **1** P **2** P   **3** N   **4** P/N

27 **Part A**: a, c

    Part B: b, c

34. Returning items

28 **(a)** Paquito   **(b)** David

    (c) Daniela   **(e)** Julieta

29 **(a)** Because they are damaged.

    (b) Exchanging them.

    (c) The receipt.

    (d) At Susana's work.

    (e) For a trip abroad.

35. Shopping opinions

30 **1** P+N **2** N   **3** P   **4** P

31 **(a)** Ana **(b)** Ana **(c)** Inés **(d)** Pablo

36. Pocket money

32 A, D, F, H

33 **1** Mario N   **2** Adriana P   **3** Merce P+N   **4** Joaquín P

37. Holiday destinations

34 **1** Manuel   **2** Enrique   **3** Luisa   **4** Clara

35 **1** E **2** A   **3** F   **4** C

38. Holiday accommodation

36 **(a)** Maruja   **(b)** Pablo

    (c) Roberto   **(d)** Juli

37 **1** Paulina D   **2** Rogelio A   **3** Samuel F   **4** Eva B

39. Booking accommodation

38 **(a)** Because they had a wonderful time before / last year.

(b) One double with bath and balcony, and one single with sea views.

(c) (i) Near / by / closer to the pool.
(ii) To be close to everything. / They can supervise their children.

(d) How much a parking space would cost.

(f) *Any two of*: Whether it's possible to bring a dog. / How much half board would cost.

40. Staying in a hotel

39 **(a)** Yulen **(b)** Sofía
(c) Benjamín **(d)** Fátima

40 **1** D **2** F **3** G **4** E

41. Staying on a campsite

41 C, F, G, H

42 **(a)** A **(b)** C **(c)** C **(d)** B

42. Holiday activities

43 **(a)** Daniela **(b)** Mario
(c) Felicia **(d)** Quique

44 **(a)** C **(b)** A **(c)** C **(d)** 4C

43. Holiday preferences

45 **(a)** J **(b)** J **(c)** M **(d)** B
(e) M **(f)** J **(g)** M **(h)** I

46 **1** Lucía P **2** David N **3** Nacho P/N

44. Future holiday plans

47 **(a)** E **(b)** B **(c)** G **(d)** A **(e)** F

48 **1** F **2** H **3** I **4** B

45. Holiday experiences

49 **(a)** C **(b)** B **(c)** B **(e)** A

50 **(a)** In a little village called Salento, in Colombia.

(b) Some very nice young people.

(c) *Any two of*: swam in the river / went fishing / cooked outside.

(d) She spent two nights sleeping with them in a cabin.

(e) Her grandmother died (shortly afterwards).

Home and environment

46. Countries and nationalities

1 **(a)** Julie **(b)** David
(c) Stacey **(d)** Jim

2 **1** G **2** E **3** F **4** D **5** B

47. My house

3 **(a)** B **(b)** A **(c)** A **(d)** C **(e)** A

4 **(a)** On the coast. / In a village.

(b) It's old and noisy.

(c) It's near the main square.

(d) *Any two of*: living room / dining room / two bedrooms.

(e) It's full of tourists in summer.

48. My room

5 **(a)** B **(b)** I **(c)** R **(d)** R
(e) I **(f)** R **(g)** I **(h)** B

6 **(a)** A **(b)** C **(c)** B **(d)** B

49. Helping at home

7 **(a) (i)** Clearing the table.
(ii) Because loading the dishwasher hurts her hands.

(b) Hoovering, because it's like doing exercise. / It's better than cleaning her room, which is boring.

(c) Walking the dog, because she hates mowing the lawn / the dog is good company / the dog is her best friend.

8 **(a)** B **(a)** B **(c)** A **(d)** A

50. My neighbourhood

9 **(a)** To tell her friend she has (just) moved away from the city.

(b) *Any two of*: little house in the country / by a forest / river in / at end of garden

(c) *Any two of*: a lot of space / fields / flowers (plant life) / fauna (wildlife / animals).

(d) Noise and pollution.

(e) Her friend coming to visit / see where she lives / and going camping.

10 **(a)** P/N **(b)** P **(c)** P/N **(d)** N **(e)** P

51. Places in town

11 **Part A**: A, D, E
Part B: A, D

12 **(a)** C **(b)** B **(c)** F **(d)** G

52. At the tourist office

13 **(a)** A **(b)** D **(c)** C **(d)** F

14 **1** A **2** C **3** B

53. Things to do in town

15 **A** N **B** N **C** P **D** N
E P/N **F** P **G** P/N **H** P

16

	Activity	Opinion
1 Laura	cultural experiences	N
2 Feliciano	flamenco shows	P
3 Margot	seeing monuments	N
4 Seve	visiting churches and mosques	N
5 Paula	eat out	P/N

54. Signs around town

17 B, D, E

18 **1** C – going shopping
2 F – meeting a friend there
3 B – staying in a hotel near there
4 E – need take out some money

55. Where I live

19 **(a)** Consuelo **(b)** Santi **(c)** Carmen
(d) Consuelo **(e)** Carmen

20 **(a)** He thinks it's okay.
(b) There are lovely views. / He loves it because he is an artist.
(c) People are very welcoming.
(d) Sometimes it can be very quiet. / There isn't much for young people to do.
(e) *Any two of*: ecological areas (in Maspalomas) / pretty beaches / restaurant (in Teror)
(f) It's made of recycled materials.
(g) Because he's interested in the environment.

56. Town description

21 **(a)** It was normal / straightforward.
(b) Of impending doom. / That something really bad was going to happen.
(c) The local mine collapsed (on 5/8/2010).
(d) The men were trapped (for 69 days).
(e) It is hard to find jobs there.
(f) **(i)** Because her uncle escaped unharmed
(ii) Because he is not going to return to the mine.
(g) He has got a job as a mechanic.

57. Weather

22 **(a)** Antonio **(b)** Isabel **(c)** María
(d) Martín **(e)** Jesús

23 **(a)** Andorra – snowy and cold
(b) Cantabria – not too cold in winter and windy
(c) México – not much rain and storms
(d) Argentina – very cold and foggy

58. Celebrations at home

24 **(a)** A **(b)** B **(c)** B **(d)** C

25 **(a)** Go to eat / have lunch at her favourite restaurant (with her mother).
(b) They had decorated the house. / There were around 40 people there for a surprise party.
(c) The band from her school who played.
(d) She says it was a wonderful day she will never forget.

59. Directions

26 **Part A**: A, C
Part B: F, B, A

27 **1** Pepe F **2** Juani A
3 Lázaro B **4** Jimena D

60. Transport

28 **Part A**: C
Part B: 1 It's the cleanest form of transport.
2 It's the cheapest form of transport
3 It's the most ecological / environmentally friendly form of transport.

29 **1** H **2** D **3** G **4** C

61. At the train station

30 **(a)** To tell Sole how to get a train ticket.
(b) A return ticket.
(c) Because she has to choose the correct town / destination / Santiago de Compostela.
(d) Because it's cheaper.
(e) Cash or credit card.
(f) He's going to wait for her on the platform.

31 **(a)** C **(b)** A **(c)** A **(d)** B

62. News headlines

32 **(a)** A **(b)** C **(c)** B **(d)** B

33 **(a)** down **(b)** up **(c)** same
(e) down **(f)** up

63. The environment

34 **(a)** A/B **(b)** A **(c)** B **(d)** A **(e)** A/B

35 **(a)** C **(b)** C **(c)** B **(d)** C

64. Environmental issues

36 **1** down **2** down **3** down **4** same

37 **(a)** A **(b)** A **(c)** A **(d)** B

65. What I do to be 'green'

38 **(a)** A **(b)** C **(c)** B **(d)** B **(e)** C

39 **(a)** G/R **(b)** G **(c)** R **(d)** G
(e) G/R **(f)** R

Work and education

66. School subjects

1 **(a)** B **(b)** C **(c)** F **(d)** D

2 B, E, G, J

67. School description

3 **(a)** E **(b)** A **(c)** B **(d)** F **(e)** K

4 **(a)** P **(b)** N **(c)** P/N **(d)** N **(e)** P
(f) P/N

68. School routine

5 **(a)** A **(b)** T **(c)** A
(d) A **(e)** S **(f)** T

6 **(a)** Tuesday.

(b) Because he didn't get up early.

(c) He talked to his friends.

(d) At home.

69. Comparing schools

7 B, C, E, H

8 B, F, H, I

70. At primary school

9 **(a)** B **(b)** G **(c)** E **(d)** K **(e)** D

10 **(a)** C **(b)** A **(c)** B **(d)** C

71. Rules at school

11 **(a)** Reason: compulsory

(b) Reason: no makeup and jewellery

(c) Rule: not to chewing gum

(d) Reason: only in the playground

(e) Reason: e-mails are allowed

(f) Rule: behaviour

12 **(a)** Switch off their mobile phones.

(b) She got a detention.

(c) During PE lessons.

(d) Running in the corridors.

(e) Silence in the library. Nobody reads there.

(f) No shouting. She agrees because it shows a lack of respect.

72. Problems at school

13 **(a)** E **(b)** D **(c)** I **(d)** G **(e)** B

14 **(a)** They have to work a lot. He will not get good marks.

(b) Lack of respect for teachers.

(c) Bullying / fights in the playground.

(d) Stress when there are important tests.

(e) Noise in class means she can't hear anything.

73. Future education plans

15 **(a)** A **(b)** C **(c)** M
(d) A **(e)** C **(f)** M

16 **(a)** maths **(b)** science **(c)** music
(d) languages **(e)** ICT

74. Future plans

17 **(a)** How difficult it was to revise so many things.

(b) B

(c) She's likes it because she gets on well with her parents. They will help her with university costs.

(d) She wants to work there because night life is great and she needs to have fun.

18 **(a)** B **(b)** A **(c)** B **(d)** C

75. Jobs

19 **(a)** A **(b)** E **(c)** H **(d)** G

20 **(a)** C **(b)** C **(c)** C **(d)** B

76. Job adverts

21 (a), (c), (f), (g)

22 **(a)** In March.

(b) Hospitality / hotel work.

(c) Willing to learn and ability to work well in a team.

(d) Flexible hours and good salary.

(e) Look on line for an application form.

77. CV

23 **(a)** She worked as a translator for five years (for different international publishing houses).

(b) In the USA.

(c) She has won several medals for sports.

(d) The headmaster of her school and the manager of the company she currently works for.

(e) She prefers working on her own.

24 **(a)** Because nowadays lots of people apply for the same job.

(b) Accurate details and your achievements / successes.

(c) With spelling and grammar.

(d) It's not a good idea. A CV needs to be appropriate for the particular job.

(e) Find out about / research the company you are going to send your CV to.

(f) You can include information that makes you seem a more attractive candidate (for prospective employers).

78. Job application

25 **(a)** In a local newspaper.

(b) In a clothes shop.

(c) She wants to work in summer because she is going to university in autumn.

(d) She did her work experience in a travel agency. / She has worked in several hotels.

(e) She has a good command of French and English.

(f) *Any one of*: hardworking / honest / punctual.

26 **(a)** 16   **(b)** waiter

(c) cookery   **(d)** hardworking and quick

79. Job interview

27 **(a)** Help two children at home.

(b) It would give her more experience with children. She wants to work as a nurse or a teacher.

(c) She arrived for the interview (fifteen minutes) early.

(d) She said that she in general she gets on with children and adults, and that she could be trusted.

(e) She was keen to get it.

28 **Part 1**:

(a) In a travel agents.

(b) Working at the airport. / Working with the public.

(c) At the local library.

Part 2:

(d) Hard working and responsible.

(e) On 16th January.

(f) The day after tomorrow.

80. Opinions about jobs

29 **(a)** B   **(b)** C   **(c)** B   **(d)** B

30 **1** E, H   **2** C, K   **3** D, G

81. Part-time jobs

31 **(a)** She hadn't expected it to be so good.

(b) She worked alone. / She was on her own.

(c) Not at all hard because she had very little work to do to during the day. / Tourists arrived early and returned the bikes late.

(d) She advised the customers on interesting places to visit.

(e) She finds it hard to be nice to children, even the spoilt ones. / She doesn't want to work as a teacher in the future.

32 **1** C   **2** D   **3** A   **4** E

82. My work experience

33 **(a)** an office

(b) bus

(c) nice / kind

(d) one week

(e) made photocopies / answered the phone / processed e-mail requests

(f) positive, but he wouldn't like to work in the company in the future

34 **1** H   **2** G   **3** E   **4** F

83. Work experience

35 **1** Ana P   **2** Paco N

3 Isabel P/N   **4** Ramón P/N

5 Pili P

36 **(a)** *Any one of*: The schedule was terrible. / The hours were long. / She found it tiring.

(b) The people she worked with for not being nice / Not getting paid.

(c) Clean and help the children.

(d) *Any two of:* To pass her exams. / To pursue a good career. / To take notice of her teachers at school.

(e) She wants to work with children – perhaps in a school.

84. Dialogues and messages

37 **Part A: (a)** A   **(b)** C   **(c)** C   **(d)** A

Part B: C, E, G, H

Grammar

Nouns and articles

1	**1** la	**2** el	**3** las	**4** los	**5** la
	6 el	**7** las	**8** los	**9** el	**10** la

2	**1** las	**2** un	**3** el	**4** los
	5 una	**6** un	**7** el	**8** El

3 **2** Mi padre es ~~un~~ dentista y mi madre es ~~una~~ enfermera.

3 Hablo ~~el~~ español y ~~el~~ sueco.

4 Escribo con ~~un~~ lápiz en mi clase de matemáticas.

5 El sábado voy a ~~la~~ casa de mis abuelos.

6 Se pueden reservar dos habitaciones con ~~una~~ ducha.

86. Adjectives

1	**1** adosada	**2** traviesos
	3 rojo	**4** interesantes
	5 español	**6** simpáticas
	7 preciosa	**8** baratos

2	**1** lujoso	**2** cómodos
	3 bueno	**4** impresionante
	5 limpia	**6** útiles

3
1 En Inglaterra hay **poca** gente que habla muy bien griego.
2 Lo mejor es que tiene un jardín **bonito**.
3 Estamos **contentas** porque hace buen tiempo.
4 En el futuro habrá una **gran** estatua aquí en la plaza.
5 Nuestro apartamento está en el **primer** piso.
6 Mis primas son **alemanas** pero viven en Escocia.

87. Possessives and pronouns

1

English	Spanish singular	Spanish plural
my	mi	**mis**
your	**tu**	tus
his / her / its	**su**	**sus**
our	**nuestro / nuestra**	nuestros / nuestras
your	**vuestro / vuestra**	**vuestros / vuestras**
their	su	**sus**

2
1 Mi   2 Su   3 Sus
4 Mis   5 Su

3
1 el mío   2 las suyas
3 el nuestro   4 el tuyo

4
1 María tiene un gato que es negro y pequeño.
2 Vivimos en un pueblo que está en el norte de Inglaterra.
3 En la clase de literatura tengo que leer un libro que es muy aburrido.

88. Comparisons

1
1 Mi madre es **más delgada que** mi padre.
2 Mariela es **menos paciente que** Francisco.
3 Este autobús es **más lento que** el tren.
4 La fruta es **tan sana / saludable como** las verduras.
5 Esta camisa es **tan cara como** aquella chaqueta.

2
1 el mejor
2 los peores
3 la más pequeña
4 los más inteligentes
5 las menos aburridas

3
1 Mi coche es el más barato.
2 Mi primo/a es más perezoso/a que tu tío.
3 Su móvil es pequeñísimo.
4 El examen de español es facilísimo.

5 Las películas de terror son tan emocionantes como las películas de acción.
6 ¡Mi instituto es el más feo!
7 Las ciencias son menos aburridas que la geografía.
8 Messi es el mejor.

89. Other adjectives

1

Masc. sing.	Fem. sing.	Masc. pl.	Fem. pl.
este	**esta**	**estos**	**estas**
ese	esa	**esos**	**esas**
aquel	**aquella**	aquellos	**aquellas**

2
1 estas botas   2 esta camiseta
3 aquella chica   4 esos plátanos
5 ese móvil   6 aquellas revistas
7 este iPod   8 esa película
9 aquel tren   10 estos sombreros
11 esas fresas   12 aquellos chicos

3
1 cada   2 misma
3 algunas   4 todos   5 mismo

4
1 Todos   2 Algunos   3 Todos
4 algunos   5 misma   6 mismos

90. Pronouns

1

yo	**I**
tú	you
él	he
ella	**she**
nosotros	we (masc.)
nosotras	**we (fem.)**
vosotros	**you (masc.)**
vosotras	you (fem.)
ellos	**they (masc.)**
ellas	they (fem.)

2
1 Las hemos perdido.
2 La han perdido.
3 Teresa lo come.
4 Lo compro.
5 No la bebo.
6 No la lavo.
7 Lo quiero escribir. / Quiero escribirlo.
8 No quiero leerla. / No la quiero leer.
9 La necesito ahora.
10 Vamos a venderla. / La vamos a vender.

3
1 I am going to call him / her this afternoon.
2 I visited them yesterday.
3 I will do it if I have time.
4 I sell them at the market.
5 Have you seen them?
6 Vino a visitarme a casa. / Me vino a visitar a casa.
7 Me mandaron la reserva.
8 Los / Las voy a comprar por Internet. / Voy a comprarlos/comprarlas por Internet.

91. The present tense

1
1 vivimos	2 bailan	3 vendo
4 lleváis	5 odias	6 come
7 salimos	8 escucha	

2
1 comen	2 vivimos	3 tienes
4 hablan	5 debe	6 grita
7 chateo	8 lee	9 piensa
10 Podéis		

3
1 cenamos	2 trabajan
3 desayuno	4 pone
5 compramos	6 cuestan
7 Quiero	8 piden

92. Reflexives and irregulars

1

me	afeito
te	afeitas
se	afeita
nos	afeitamos
os	afeitáis
se	afeitan
me	visto
te	vistes
se	viste
nos	vestimos
os	vestís
se	visten

2
1 se	2 se	3 te
4 se	5 se	6 Nos
7 Os	8 Te	

3 Todos los días Olivia **se levanta** temprano para ir a trabajar. **Trabaja** en una tienda de ropa famosa. Primero **se lava** los dientes y luego **se ducha** y **se viste**. **Baja** las escaleras y **desayuna** cereales con fruta. Siempre **se peina** en la cocina. Después, **se lava** la cara en el cuarto de baño que está abajo, al lado de la cocina. **Se pone** la chaqueta y **sale** a las ocho y media porque el autobús llega a las nueve menos cuarto. **Vuelve** a casa a las siete de la tarde.

93. *Ser* and *estar*

1
1 está	2 son	3 Soy	4 es
5 Son	6 está	7 Estáis	
8 Estamos			

2
1 Where is the bank? ("estar" for location)
2 My grandmothers are very generous. ("ser" for characteristics)
3 I am from Madrid but I work in Barcelona. ("ser" for where you are from)
4 The dress is green with white flowers. ("ser" for colours)
5 It's four thirty in the afternoon. ("ser" for time)
6 The wardrobe is opposite the door. ("estar" for location)
7 You are (all) very sad today because the holidays have finished. ("estar" for moods)
8 We are ready for the drama exam. ("estar" for meaning "ready" not "clever")

3
1, 4, 5, 7 – ✓
2 Mi amigo **es** inteligente y tiene el pelo negro.
3 Me duele la cabeza y **estoy** enfermo.
6 Mi madre **es** dependienta y mi padre **es** ingeniero.
8 Mi casa **es** bastante pequeña – tiene solo un dormitorio.

94. The gerund

1
1 comiendo – eating
2 saltando – jumping
3 corriendo – runnning
4 tomando – taking (drinking / eating)
5 durmiendo – sleeping
6 asistiendo – attending
7 escribiendo - writing
8 escuchando – listening
9 aprendiendo – learning
10 pudiendo – being able to

2
1 Está montando en bicicleta.
2 Estoy escuchando música.
3 Están navegando por Internet.
4 Estamos viendo una película.
5 Estás hablando con amigos.

3
1 Estaba haciendo vela cuando llegó la tormenta.

2 Estaban comiendo cuando su madre les llamó.

3 Estábamos tomando el sol cuando empezó a llover.

4 Estabas cantando cuando salió el tren.

5 Estábamos viendo la tele cuando nuestro padre volvió a casa.

6 Estaba jugando a los videojuegos cuando llamó.

7 Estabais escuchando al profesor cuando entró el perro.

8 Estaba nadando en el mar cuando el tiburón apareció.

95. The preterite tense

1
1	sacaron	**2**	volvimos	**3**	compró
4	llegaste	**5**	trabajasteis	**6**	fue
7	di	**8**	tuvimos	**9**	visitaron
10	bebió				

2
1	fui	**2**	tuvimos	**3**	dieron
4	fue	**5**	me levanté, me vestí		
6	hicieron	**7**	dijo	**8**	fue
9	Hice	**10**	tuve		

3 **Fui** al cine con mis amigos y **vimos** una película de acción. Después **comimos** en un restaurante italiano. **Comí** una pizza con jamón y queso, y mi amiga Lola **comió** pollo con pasta. **Bebimos** zumo de manzana y mi amigo Tom **comió** tarta de chocolate pero yo no **comí** postre. Después del restaurante **fui** en tren a casa de mi prima. El viaje **fue** largo y aburrido. **Volví** a casa y me **acosté** a las once de la noche.

96. The imperfect tense

2 De pequeños <u>nadábamos</u> en el mar todas las semanas. ✓

3 <u>Había</u> mucha gente en el museo y las estatuas <u>eran</u> preciosas. ✓

5 Cuando <u>eran</u> pequeños, no <u>comían</u> tomate ni lechuga.

8 Me <u>ponía</u> nervioso cada vez que <u>hacía</u> una prueba de vocabulario. ✓

10 <u>Nevaba</u> todos los días y <u>hacía</u> un frío horrible. ✓

2
1 Last Wednesday we went to the swimming pool and we swam for an hour and a half. (preterite for a completed action in the past)

2 When we were kids, we used to swim in the sea every week. (imperfect for "used to")

3 There were lots of people in the museum and the statues were beautiful. (imperfect for descriptions)

4 My father prepared a vegetarian supper for us. (preterite for a completed action in the past)

5 When they were younger, they didn't eat tomatoes or lettuce. (imperfect to describe repeated actions in the past)

6 Gabriela arrived in Madrid by train to start her new job. (preterite for a completed action in the past)

7 Yesterday we met in the café and we talked all afternoon. (preterite for a completed action in the past)

8 I used to get nervous every time I did a vocabulary test. (imperfect for "used to")

9 I had a great time because it was sunny and it didn't rain. (preterite for a completed action in the past)

10 It snowed every day and it was terribly cold. (imperfect for descriptions)

3
1	tenía	**2**	vivía	**3**	Estaba
4	pasé	**5**	trabajaban	**6**	gastó
7	comíamos	**8**	jugué		

97. The future tense

1
1	jugar	**2**	Va	**3**	a	**4**	voy
5	Vas	**6**	Vais	**7**	va	**8**	ir
9	vamos	**10**	Voy				

2
1 Vamos a ver la película.

2 No trabajaré los lunes.

3 Van a coger el metro.

4 Irá a Inglaterra.

5 Van a jugar con mi hermano.

6 Irás a España.

3
1	va a ir	**2**	voy a ir
3	voy a tomar	**4**	voy a tener
5	Voy a trabajar	**6**	Va a ser
7	va a ser	**8**	va a seguir
9	va a vivir		

98. The conditional

1
1 compraríamos – we would buy

2 saldrían – they would go out

3 trabajaríais – you (all) would work

4 estaría – he / she / it would be

5 jugarías – you would play

6 vendríamos – we would come

7 podrías – you could

8 habría – there would be

2
1	iría	**2**	tomarían
3	trabajaría	**4**	ganaríamos
5	habría	**6**	usaría
7	malgastarían	**8**	lucharían
9	ganaría	**10**	compartiríamos

3 NB All answers can use either *podrías* or *deberías*. Some answers are interchangeable.
1 Podrías evitar el estrés.
2 Podrías comer más fruta y verduras.
3 Deberías hacer más ejercicio.
4 Deberías ir al médico.
5 Deberías acostarte temprano.
6 Podrías ir al dentista.
7 Deberías consumir menos energía.
8 Podrías comprar ropa de segunda mano.

99. Perfect and pluperfect

1

Perfect tense	Pluperfect tense
he	**había**
has	**habías**
ha	había
hemos	**habíamos**
habéis	**habíais**
han	habían

2 **1** We have lost our car.
2 Have you studied Spanish?
3 They have bought a laptop.
4 I have done my homework
5 We have seen a very informative documentary.
6 Me he roto el brazo.
7 Han perdido la maleta.
8 Hemos comido muchos caramelos.
9 ¿Has visitado el museo hoy?
10 El dependiente / La dependienta ha abierto la tienda.
3 **2** había perdido **3** había nadado
4 había ido **5** había dejado
6 había encontrado

100. Giving instructions

1 **1** Dobla a la derecha.
2 Cruza la plaza.
3 Pasa el puente.
4 Ten cuidado.
5 Ven aquí.
6 Canta más bajo.
7 Lee en voz alta.
8 Escucha bien.
9 Pon la mesa.
10 Haz este ejercicio.
2 **1** Doblad a la derecha.
2 Cruzad la plaza.
3 Pasad el puente.
4 Tened cuidado.
5 Venid aquí.
6 Cantad más bajo.
7 Leed en voz alta.

8 Escuchad bien
9 Poned la mesa.
10 Haced este ejercicio.
3 **1** ¡Descarga la música!
2 ¡Doblad a la izquierda!
3 ¡Quita la mesa!
4 ¡Haz la cama!
5 ¡Pasad la aspiradora!

101. The present subjunctive

1 **1** hable **2** coman **3** vaya
4 vivas **5** trabajéis **6** salga
7 pueda **8** hagan **9** encuentre
10 seamos
2 **1** No comas este pastel.
2 No compres aquel vestido.
3 No tomes estas pastillas.
4 No bebas un vaso de zumo de naranja.
5 No veas esta película romántica.
6 No firmes aquí.
7 No rellenes el formulario.
8 No saltes tres veces.
3 **1** trabajen **2** haga **3** tengamos
4 sean **5** vaya **6** compren

102. Negatives

1 **1** No estudio geografía.
2 No vamos a las afueras.
3 Ricardo no compró una moto nueva.
4 Sus padres no vieron la tele.
5 No voy a ir a Francia la semana que viene.
2 **1** e **2** d **3** b **4** g
5 a/f **6** a/f **7** c
3 **1** Mis profesores no enseñan nunca cómo teclear.
2 En mi casa no tuvimos jamás una sala de juegos.
3 No me he quemado nunca los brazos.
4 Aquí no tengo ni vestidos, ni faldas, ni camisetas.
5 No vas a comprar ningún coche.
6 Mis padres no escuchan a nadie.
4 **1** Por la tarde nunca bebemos / tomamos café. / Por la tarde no bebemos / tomamos nunca café.
2 No plancho, ni cocino, ni limpio.
3 No hablan ningún idioma.
4 No podemos hablar con nadie durante el examen.
5 No fumaré jamás / nunca porque es una pérdida de tiempo. / Jamás / Nunca fumaré porque es una pérdida de tiempo.

103. Special verbs

1

me		I like
te		you like
le	gusta (sing.)	he / she / it likes
nos	gustan (plural)	we like
os		you (all) like
les		they like

2 1, 3 – ✓
  2 Nos **apetece** ir al teatro mañana.
  4 No nos **gusta** la contaminación atmosférica.
  5 ¿Te **hacen** falta unas toallas?

3 **1** Nos hace falta un abrigo.
  2 Os encantan los caballos negros.
  3 A María le gustan aquellos zapatos.
  4 Te quedan veinte euros para comprar el regalo.
  5 Me duele la garganta todo el tiempo.
  6 Les encantan los rascacielos porque son modernos.

104. *Por* and *para*

1 **1** For my birthday I want a new mobile phone.
  2 My friend works for a lawyer.
  3 Apps for the iPhone are incredible.
  4 I eat a lot of vegetables and fish in order to keep fit.
  5 You need the key to get into the house.
  6 Smoking is very bad for your health.
  7 They are going to organise a party to celebrate the end of the course.
  8 For me, sports are always fun.

2 **1** El coche rojo pasó por las calles antiguas.
  2 Normalmente por la mañana me gusta desayunar cereales y fruta.
  3 Mandé la reserva por correo electrónico.
  4 Me gustaría cambiar este jersey por otro.
  5 En la tienda ganamos diez euros por hora.
  6 Había mucha basura por todas partes.

3 **1** Para **2** para **3** por
  4 para **5** para

105. Questions and exclamations

1 Why? – ¿Por qué?
  What? – ¿Qué?
  When? – ¿Cuándo?
  How? – ¿Cómo?
  Where? – ¿Dónde?
  Where to? – ¿Adónde?
  Which? – ¿Cuál?
  Which ones? – ¿Cuáles?
  How much? – ¿Cuánto?
  How many? – ¿Cuántos?

2 **1** F **2** E **3** G **4** J **5** A **6** C **7** I
  8 B **9** H **10** D

3 **1** horror **2** Cuánto **3** Dónde
  4 guay **5** rollo

106. Connectives and adverbs

1 **1** rápidamente **2** difícilmente
  3 lentamente **4** alegremente
  5 tranquilamente

2 **1** L **2** E **3** A **4** K **5** D **6** B
  7 G **8** J **9** F **10** I **11** C **12** H

3 **1** Sus padres cantan mal en la iglesia.
  2 No hablo mucho porque soy tímido.
  3 El tren pasa rápidamente por el túnel.
  4 Los pendientes son demasiado caros.
  5 A menudo comemos huevos por la mañana. / Comemos a menudo huevos por la mañana.
  6 si / porque
  7 porque
  8 pero

107. Numbers

1
A	veinte 20		**L**	quinientos 500
B	cuarenta y ocho 48		**M**	un millón 1000000
C	nueve 9		**N**	novecientos 900
D	cien 100		**O**	ochenta y ocho 88
E	catorce 14		**P**	setenta y seis 76
F	mil 1000		**Q**	sesenta y siete 67
G	trescientos 300		**R**	diez 10
H	cincuenta y siete 57		**S**	cero 0
I	veintitrés 23		**T**	veintinueve 29
J	quince 15			
K	diecinueve 19			

2 **1** mil novecientos noventa y nueve
  2 el diez de octubre
  3 el primero/uno de enero
  4 el tres de marzo
  5 dos mil trece
  6 el dieciséis de noviembre
  7 el treinta de mayo
  8 mil novecientos sesenta y ocho
  9 dos mil dos
  10 el veintiuno de abril

3 **1** 20, 25 € veinte euros con veinticinco
  2 59, 10 € cincuenta y nueve euros con diez
  3 100,75 € cien euros con setenta y cinco
  4 87 € ochenta y siete euros
  5 45,20 € cuarenta y cinco euros con veinte
  6 7,99 € siete euros con noventa y nueve
  7 86,70 € ochenta y seis euros con setenta
  8 30,65 € treinta euros con sesenta y cinco

Practice Exam Paper

108. Reading

1   **1** B   **2** A   **3** E   **4** C

2   **(a)** Chus   **(b)** Juan
       (c) Nando   **(d)** Elvira
       (e) Fátima

3   **(a)** Antonio   **(b)** Isabel
       (c) Martín   **(d)** Mar
       (e) Ángel

4   **(a)** Paragraph 1 – E
       (b) Paragraph 2 – B
       (c) Paragraph 3 – C

5   **(a)** B   **(b)** C   **(c)** B   **(d)** B

6   B, C, D, H

7   C, D, F, H

8   **(a)** His parents were successful / successful sports people.

       (b) He has impaired vision.

       (c) He has difficulty reading small print. / He has difficulty leaving the house / walking.

       (d) He has won several medals

       (e) Displayed all his medals somewhere everyone can see them.

       (f) Determination, sense of responsibility and enthusiasm

9   **(a)** E – Talk to your parents. Explain what is annoying you and listen to their complaints.

       (b) B – Discuss with your friends things to do that don't cost much.

       (c) D – Study hard and do extracurricular activities. That will help to have an interesting CV.

       (e) C – Join a local club where they practice sports or do other activities she likes. She'll make friends.

115. Listening

1   **1** A   **2** C   **3** D   **4** F

2   **(a)** Ana   **(b)** David   **(c)** Conchi
       (d) David

3   **1** D – N
       2 E – P
       3 H – N
       4 A – P

4   **(a)** C   **(b)** B   **(c)** A   **(d)** A

5   B, C, E, H

6   **(a)** B   **(b)** C   **(c)** A   **(d)** C   **(e)** A

7   **(a)** The (Estrella) Club is opening.

       (b) There is an open day / day for visitors /

prospective members.

       (c) Two swimming pools, one indoors and the other an outdoor Olympic-sized pool.

       (d) Not as much as you think.

       (e) Presents / a big discount.

       (f) Activities for all the family. / A shop selling sporting equipment at good price.

8

Positive aspects
(a) you make new friends / can communicate with your loved ones
(b) you can find out how to do things
(c) helps with homework
(d) is an interesting pastime

Negative aspects
(a) can be addictive
(b) can be unsafe
(c) sometimes is unreliable
(d) makes people unfriendly / kills the art of conversation

9   **(a)** He was knocked off his bike by a car.

       (b) Broken leg / liver damage.

       (c) Long waits and not enough beds.

       (d) He had a heart attack.

       (e) Likes it.

Your own notes

Your own notes

Published by Pearson Education Limited, Edinburgh Gate, Harlow, Essex, CM20 2JE.

www.pearsonschoolsandfecolleges.co.uk

Text © Pearson Education Limited 2013
Audio recorded at Tom Dick + Debbie Productions, © Pearson Education Limited
MFL Series Editor Julie Green
Edited by Ruth Manteca, Tracy Traynor and Sue Chapple
Typeset by Kamae Design, Oxford
Original illustrations © Pearson Education Limited 2013
Illustrations by KJA Artists, John Hallett
Cover illustration by Miriam Sturdee

The rights of Jacqueline López-Cascante and Leanda Reeves to be identified as authors of this work have been asserted by them in accordance with the Copyright, Designs and Patents Act 1988.

First published 2013

16 15
10 9 8 7 6 5 4 3

British Library Cataloguing in Publication Data
A catalogue record for this book is available from the British Library

ISBN 978 1 447 94122 4

Printed in Slovakia by Neografia

Acknowledgements

The publisher would like to thank the following for their kind permission to reproduce their photographs:

(Key: b-bottom; c-centre; l-left; r-right; t-top)
Creatas: 62; Pearson Education Ltd: Studio 8 42/1, 42/3, 48tl, Gareth Boden 42/5, 48r, Handan Erek 32cl, 42/2, 42/4; Shutterstock.com: pio3 36; Veer/Corbis: fotovincek 32tr, PT images 32r, SasPartout 32tl

All other images © Pearson Education Limited

Every effort has been made to contact copyright holders of material reproduced in this book. Any omissions will be rectified in subsequent printings if notice is given to the publishers.

In the writing of this book, no AQA examiners authored sections relevant to examination papers for which they have responsibility.